Derek O'Brien was born in Kolkata. He began his professional career as a journalist for *Sportsworld* magazine but soon shifted to advertising. After working for a number of very successful years as Creative Head of Ogilvy, Derek decided to focus all his energy and talent in his passion—quizzing.

Today, Derek O'Brien is Asia's best-known quizmaster and the CEO of Derek O'Brien & Associates. He is the host of the longest-running game show on Indian television, the Bournvita Quiz Contest, for which he was voted the Best Anchor of a Game Show at the Indian Television Academy Awards for three years in a row. He also hosts the longest-running corporate quiz show, the Economic Times Brand Equity Quiz. Always innovating and keeping abreast with the times, he is also credited with having conducted the first quiz on Twitter in 2010.

Derek O'Brien has written over forty best-selling reference and quiz books.

In 2011, he was voted to the Rajya Sabha as a Member of Parliament and is the Chief Whip of the Trinamool Congress in the Rajya Sabha and is also the national spokesperson of the party. In 2012, he had the honour of addressing the UN General Assembly.

Stay in touch with Derek on Twitter (his handle is @quizderek) or through the Derek O'Brien & Associates website www.derek.in.

Other books by Derek O'Brien
(from Rupa Publications)

Bournvita Quiz Contest Quiz Book 2012
Ultimate BQC Book of Knowledge (Volumes 1 and 2)
The Best of Bournvita Quiz Contest
Derek's Challenge
Speak Up, Speak Out:
My Favourite Elocution Pieces and How to Deliver Them

Success Mantras of 12 Achievers

Edited by
Derek O'Brien

First published by
Rupa Publications India Pvt. Ltd 2014
7/16, Ansari Road, Daryaganj
New Delhi 110002

Sales Centres:

Allahabad Bengaluru Chennai
Hyderabad Jaipur Kathmandu
Kolkata Mumbai

Introduction, chapter introductions and chapter 13 copyright
© Derek O'Brien & Associates 2014

Copyright for individual pieces vests with the authors
Page 141 is an extension of the copyright page

All rights reserved.
No part of this publication may be reproduced, transmitted,
or stored in a retrieval system, in any form or by any means,
electronic, mechanical, photocopying, recording or otherwise,
without the prior permission of the publisher.

ISBN: 978-81-291-3088-4

Second impression 2014

10 9 8 7 6 5 4 3 2

The moral right of the author has been asserted.

Printed by Thomson Press India Ltd, Faridabad

Not for sale in the United Kingdom.

This book is sold subject to the condition that it shall not,
by way of trade or otherwise, be lent, resold, hired out, or otherwise circulated,
without the publisher's prior consent, in any form of binding or cover other
than that in which it is published.

To Tonuca

Contents

Introduction   *ix*

1. In Pursuit of Perfection   3
   Abhinav Bindra
2. Success Comes from Will-power   15
   Akio Morita
3. How to Succeed in Life   21
   Andrew Carnegie
4. I Succeeded Because I Failed   27
   A.P.J. Abdul Kalam
5. Perseverance Can Make Miracles Happen   41
   Azim Premji
6. How to be the Greatest Doctor   53
   Dr Devi Shetty
7. Never Give Up   65
   Donald Trump
8. My Passion Keeps Me Going   73
   Leander Paes
9. Cricket, the Mind Game   85
   Mahendra Singh Dhoni
10. 10 Life Lessons   95
    N.R. Narayana Murthy

11. It's All About Hard Work *Saina Nehwal*	105
12. Enjoy this Second Chance *Salman 'Sal' Khan*	117
13. Learning from Mother Teresa *Derek O'Brien*	131
Acknowledgements	141

Introduction

What is success? Is it an overrated emotion? Is it the natural goal of all human pursuit? Is it too personal to describe or ascribe as a general phenomenon? Is it measurable in numbers: rupees and dollars, metres and miles, square feet and column inches? This book is a means to find out. It is not so much a road-map for attaining success as an exploration of the idea of success, told through and by people who are recognized as successful.

The heroes in this book come from various fields. On the face of it, many of them have little in common other than the fact that they are well-known names and easily identified faces. That aside, they represent a divergence of nationalities and ethnicities, experiences and callings. Andrew Carnegie was a steel magnate and philanthropist in nineteenth-century America; Leander Paes is an extraordinarily durable tennis player in the second decade of the twenty-first century. What could they possibly share other than a quest for excellence?

Success is too easily correlated to intelligence, scholastic achievement and hard work. This is true but only up to a point. Azim Premji puts it lyrically when he says perseverance can make miracles happen. Yet, perseverance in which direction and to what end? Many people work hard, but not all of them become successful. There is obviously some other ingredient in this recipe for success—whether in producing great art, setting up massive industrial facilities, running faster than the competition on the track, or invoking the appropriate emotion on camera.

It is this mystical quality—this intangible—that helps some of humankind make the leap from effort to success. It is this attribute that we seek to examine and interrogate in the coming pages.

The ingredients of success are varied and change from individual to individual. Indeed, the roots of success may lie in experiences that are anything but successful. Donald Trump explains this striking paradox. A man so associated with over-the-top flamboyance and the high life, Trump focuses, while writing on the architecture of success, on failure: on the lowest point, the turning point, on how failure is not permanent. Reading this set me thinking. Everybody fails at some point or the other, but those who eventually succeed just tackle that failure differently.

To succeed you need to fail

Basketball legend Michael Jordan famously said: 'I have missed more than 9,000 shots in my career. I have lost almost 300 games. On twenty-six occasions I have been entrusted to take the game-winning shot, and I have missed. I have failed over and over in my life. And that is why I succeed.' They say statistics don't obsess the truly great sportspersons, but here was perhaps the finest basketball player of all time, reeling off figures related to the times he had let down his team and his talent. In a sense, Jordan was reminding us of one of life's simple rules: we all have to fail.

Even the people who are seemingly the most successful do not walk the journey of life without tripping, without making that one colossal blunder. Winston Churchill is known for his wartime leadership in World War II. Thirty years earlier, he was known for his wartime failure in proposing the disastrous Dardanelles Campaign, one of the tragedies of World War I. How did Churchill turn his destiny a hundred and eighty degrees? He drew the right lessons from his failure. Failure is not a problem if one learns from it.

Empirical evidence bears this out. Most successful people who have experienced failure have done so in the first thirty or so years of their life. To go back to the Churchill example, he was forty when World War I broke out. Early failure, like an early mistake in a long-distance race, gives you the time to recover. Physically and psychologically, it is easier for the young to bounce back from failure; they still have a lifetime ahead to make amends.

Can success be planned?

No one plans failure but can one plan success? There are those who say they had their lives and attainments and successes chalked out the moment they entered high school, and had their career graphs charted on the second day in management school. Those boasts sound nice; they are about as real as fairy tales. True, success can stem from self-confidence and early ideation but it cannot be divorced from instinct and effort, creativity and imagination and the search for happiness.

To my mind, success is also inextricably linked to the process of creation—creating a song or a book, an engineering product or a company, a brand or even creating, if that be the word, an inspired chess move from the recesses of the mind. The relationship between a creator and his or her creation is that between a mother and her child. Some of these relationships and some of these mothers/creators and children/creations are more successful or better rounded or just happier and more satisfied than others. This analogy may sound forced, but is it really? This brings us to another subject—the emotions of success.

The emotions of success

Two people could start off from similar backgrounds, have matching career profiles and earn the same amount each month, doing pretty much the same thing. Nevertheless, it is possible that one of the two persons would deem himself successful and satisfied, and the other would consider himself a failure, restless and still far from his benchmarks of success. Success then is about going on, but also about knowing when to stop. It is, as a friend put it to me so beautifully, all about 'that quest for happiness'.

Success is about caring too; it is the ultimate in people skills. Dr Devi Shetty puts it remarkably when he says: 'Be humble, be polite, it doesn't cost you anything to be nice to others. As doctors, people touch our feet, they think we are God. They make us feel that we're not ordinary, but remember we are like anybody else.'

As we can see, success has many elements. It is a meeting of mind and soul, both a science and an art; it requires a clinical brain as much as it needs a warm heart.

Success is about people

My first boss and editor at *Sportsworld* magazine was Mansur Ali Khan Pataudi. He was a successful cricket captain not because he led the most successful team in the world, the one that won the most matches—actually India didn't win many games in the 1960s. He was a successful editor not because his magazine broke Pulitzer-winning stories and sold a million copies a week. 'Tiger', as the aristocratic Pataudi was universally known, was successful primarily because he treated people, his fellow cricketers or his journalist colleagues, as his biggest assets, invested in them a certain sense of belonging and dignity, and made them proud of being part of a team: *his* team.

In time the outer accoutrements of success came to those cricketers and those novice journalists. To many of them it didn't matter. Pataudi had made them feel successful years before external observers decided to label them thus. Leander Paes, another great Indian sportsperson, would nod to this. To him, '[Success is] surrounding yourself with a good team, surrounding yourself with good quality people, their skills don't have to match, their passion and their enthusiasm for excellence need to match.'

Making the selection

This introduction offers only a snapshot of the riches that lie in the rest of the book. It cannot and does not pretend to represent every person, every irrepressible character in the coming pages.

Each life is a parable, each one so different—and yet so alike.

While choosing the pieces for this book I had one thing in mind—the lyrics of a song I grew up listening to. It is 'My Way', written by Paul Anka and made famous by the legendary Frank Sinatra. The words of the song say it all: the ambition, the setbacks, the joys and the tragedies that each of the persons in the following pages has faced—yet they have done it all in their own special way.

This book just had to be called *My Way*.

Sports is success in its purest form

The pieces and the icons I have chosen to include in this book are inevitably a reflection of my personal beliefs and value systems. Discerning readers will detect a high proportion of sportspersons. This represents the sports lover in me and also an unrequited ambition to make it big in sport. Years ago, I was captain of my school soccer team, the goalkeeper and pivot. I nursed ambitions of playing for India and did play league football in Kolkata, learning at the feet—or from the feet—of giants of Indian football in those days.

Football taught me a lot: discipline and commitment, camaraderie and level-headedness, the sobriety of humility and the seductiveness of hubris, anticipation and quick thinking, physical fitness, and taking loss in one's stride. I had to overcome my physical handicaps, playing with a bandana holding back my glasses. I never made it big as a footballer, turning instead to sports writing for my first job and continuing my worship of sport in another form. To me sport represented, and continues to represent, nobility and endeavour, hope and pride, and success in its purest form.

On the sports field, you have a fixed mission. All you are looking at is the ball heading your way that you need to stop, or to get it through the hoop, or to read its movement and strike it with the bat. On the field, a lot of life's unnecessary complications fall by the wayside. Objectives are defined clearly—identify your ambition, play for the team, trust your instincts, overcome failures by looking ahead, take setbacks in your stride. These attributes are astonishingly similar to what any so-called self-help book will tell you. Sport is a self-help guide in motion; literally.

Where are the female icons in the book?

Reading the manuscript, a friend told me he was surprised by the small number of women in the list of the successful people featured. Actually, there is just one woman, the badminton player and Olympic medallist Saina Nehwal. I pondered this and sensed the reason I had not consciously looked for female icons just to reach some sort of forced balance was because five of the six biggest influences in my life have been women.

The one male who influenced me was and is my father, Neil O'Brien, who bore early setbacks in life, personal and financial, with a dignity and a bearing that was unusual, who never let this interfere with his quest for knowledge, and never chased the outwardly glorious for the inwardly meaningful. He refused a nomination to Parliament because it would force him to resign from his job at Oxford University Press and not take the position of managing director, which meant a lot to him and was to him the pinnacle of a lifetime of striving. He did finally go to Parliament, but only after ending his publishing career.

The five women who influenced my life

The first big female influence on my life has been that of my mother, Joyce. She loves me, like all mothers love their sons, but best of all she has taught me to tackle failure, to get up, dust myself and run on. In class eight I had been kept back at St. Xavier's, Kolkata. I had moved mid-year from St. Columba's, Delhi, as my father had been transferred from Delhi to Kolkata. The coursework and academic schedules didn't match and I found myself unable to keep up with my classmates.

Those excuses sound fine in hindsight. At the time it happened, and the report card came in, it was crushing. That afternoon my mother did something unusual. She took the family out to lunch. I remember we went to Waldorf, an old Chinese restaurant in Kolkata for what would have appeared to be a celebration. She told me the coming year would be easy enough for me because I had made myself familiar with my books anyway, and could expect to do much better than my classmates. 'It'll be easy for you, son,' she said, 'don't worry.'

There was a mother's indulgence in that conversation but also a steely will. She was motivating me to do much better the following year, had more or less told me I had the tools and the experience to do well and indicated that success was obvious if I worked honestly for it, and that I would have no excuses in twelve months. Best of all, it was all conveyed with a smile and in an easy manner, over a family dinner.

The second big female influence is that of my wife, Tonuca. From her I've learnt the skill of prioritising, of determination and of commitment. We have a long-distance marriage. She is a doctor and a mother in New York, caring for her daughters from a previous marriage. She is determined to make our marriage work and her career work, to do her duty to her children and find time for companionship with her husband. It's not easy, but to Tonuca it's a no-brainer—it has to be done and done smoothly. She needs to be in New York till her girls go to college in 2017; she owes them that.

So we meet every eight weeks, making trips to each other's cities, chalking up—and using—frequent flyer miles and appreciating each other that much more, I would imagine, than if we woke up in the same house 365 days a year. To juggle three different commitments—as a mother, a wife and a doctor—and to make a mark in all three, when de-prioritising one or even two would have been so tempting, is a hallmark of success. Tonuca has taught me a lot.

The third big female influence is that of my daughter, Aanya. She has the uncomplicated honesty and the brutal frankness of youth. She is my worst, or best, critic. If I'm not looking good on stage or the way I delivered my speech in Parliament had some shortcomings, she will tell me. If my clothes sense sometimes fails me, Aanya lets me know. In her own way, she keeps me grounded and I have started valuing her opinion. Realizing her opinion matters to me she has, showing a maturity beyond her years, begun to offer it with particular thought and integrity. She also keeps me contemporary, I often joke, by introducing me to new trends in music.

The fourth big female influence in my life was that of my former wife, Rila Banerjee. In 1991, I left a secure job because an entrepreneurial bug bit me. She encouraged me to believe in the idea, when it was only an idea. Risk taking is important for success. After all, even Edmund Hillary named his autobiography *Nothing Venture, Nothing Win*!

The final female influence in my life is that of Mamata Banerjee, Chief Minister of West Bengal. She is the older sister I never had, a friend, mentor, guide and leader. From her, I imbibed the merits of conviction and resilience. When she began her independent political career in the mid-1990s, nobody gave her a ghost of a chance. In time, she built a career, built a party, built a movement, and built a mandate. Now she is determined to (re)build a society at peace with itself.

Friends, each of the six influences—five of them women—from my life I have written about in the preceding paragraphs has taught me something different. Each of them represents a different set of qualities. Those qualities come together in an intricate matrix—a matrix that spells success.

I hope you enjoy the rest of the book.

Derek O'Brien

1

Winning is important, but, the journey is more meaningful. The constant pursuit toward overcoming one's own limitations and always challenging the part of you that says you will not or cannot win... My advice is enjoy the ride. Let's face it, roller coasters are far more thrilling than merry-go-rounds.

ABHINAV BINDRA

∽

Abhinav Bindra's journey to becoming India's first individual Olympic and World Championship gold medallist is a story of single-minded passion and an obsession for perfection. Shattered by his failure at the 2004 Athens Olympics, he picked himself up and moved forward with determination and grit, trying everything and anything to improve his mind, body and spirit to win that gold that had eluded him so far. In his pursuit of perfection he soled his shoes with rubber from Ferrari tyres, drank yak's milk, underwent commando training, mapped his own brain and even practised in the dark.

If you want an example of how meticulous planning and back-breaking hours of hard work can lead to perfection, look no further.

Through these excerpts from his autobiography, *A Shot at*

History, you will get to understand the true grit of a champion and the hard work and years of training that it takes to become one. You will get to understand the dedication and the lengths to which Bindra went to ensure that he would not repeat the disappointment of the 2004 Olympics. Bindra shows us that Indians can be world beaters if only we develop a die-hard attitude and a focused desire to be the best.

∽

In Pursuit of Perfection
Abhinav Bindra

I hated physical sports

I was a fat boy, a normal gregarious kid, who wasn't keen on reading, hated physical activity and was ambivalent about playing sport. Physical training classes were akin to hard labour and I would find the flimsiest excuse to bunk them.

My father, bless him, tried. Every day I was in Doon School, he wrote me a letter. His letters had one common theme: try sport, son. Dad tried. He pushed. It didn't work. And then I found something else.

Guns. I was about ten when my father first allowed me to shoot. He held the shotgun, I pulled the trigger. Quick to sense my fascination, he gifted me air guns on my birthdays. The individuality and solitude of shooting, the reality that any success or failure rested entirely with me, was intriguing. I began to get a strange sensation, as though this was something I was meant to do.

Defeat and despair at Athens

All defeat haunts, but this one, in the final of the 10-metre air-rifle event at the 2004 Olympics cut deeper. It seemed to infect my nervous system, worming into my brain and flooding it with worthlessness. It devastated me and stirred me to anger. The dreams of that final have gone away, but not what Athens did to me. This is where my life turned.

History. It's what I came to make in Athens. History is not what I shot, but history was also partially my fuel. I guess I had the power to alter that, I presume people believed I had the power to change that. Now I'd failed.

Moving forward with determination

It's 5 a.m. Winter. Chandigarh, 2005. It's cold it's dark, I don't want to get up. I am a shooter, I stand still for a living, why do I need to run? Rise, I fall back on my pillow. I hate running, especially on a treadmill. It's as monotonous as shooting. No, it's worse.

But I need it, being fit gives me confidence, it builds my self-esteem. I need to know I did everything to be the best, whether it concerns my gun, my nutrition, my technique, my brain, my body. So I must push myself to the extremities of my being. Every single day. I have to make my life difficult, break it down into minute detail and master each part.

I do this because of that Olympic medal out there, that elusive circular piece of metal at the end of a ribbon, which means the world to me. All I know is that I want it like an ache. So I rise, pull on my shorts, lace my shoes, go out into the dark and the cold. And I wear out my treadmill.

My obsession with perfection

Obsession is the child of ambition; it is also born sometimes from the need for redemption. But obsession also arrives from the fact that flawlessness is possible in shooting. Obsession, in a way, is the journey to perfection. I will do anything to be better than the rest, I have to be better. And so I go and get a lipo-dissolve done in Australia just to help my shooting. A fat-dissolving substance was injected into my hip through a hundred very painful pricks. It swelled up, I got a fever, but it worked. The second day I shot a 600 and I thought, this is it, I've got it. The next day, damn, the 9s were back.

Failure of this experiment was hardly a deterrence. Between 2004 and 2008, I experimented like a hippie from the 1960s. It was a pure pursuit of perfection, a calibrated hunt for anything that could assist my quest for a flawless performance by half a per cent. It was a need to isolate every variable, to control every aspect of performance, to break it down into hundreds of tiny, perfect parts. Not every vitamin injection I took, not every bottle of yak milk drunk, bullet chosen, jacket redesigned, was going to help. I knew that, but I was playing a mental game with myself.

Journey to Beijing—the places I went to in an attempt to improve:

Dry firing in dark room (2005)

I stand in the dark, gun in firing position, and concentrate, and it gives me awareness of my balance and stability. I sense my body more acutely, I am more alert and conscious of my muscles.

Twenty sessions in a Samadhi Tank (2008)

During the time it takes me to shoot, maybe 10 seconds, maybe 75, my mind cannot stutter or shift. The Samadhi Tank is a floatation tank, a capsule, where you are deprived of light. You lie in 10 cm of water to which is added roughly 200 kg of Epsom salts to make it buoyant. It's a fine place to meditate and visualize. I did about twenty sessions, many in the last month before the Beijing Olympics.

Designing the ideal shooting jacket (2005-07)

My jacket, pockmarked with holes, looks like it's been attacked by an irate grandmother with a knitting needle. My elbow bounces off the material, so puncturing the jacket has eased the effect. I also got a tailor in Chandigarh to design a jacket. I think he went insane because I'd keep saying, 'Arre, it's 5 mm off here, too tight by 3 mm here,' until he realized I was looking for impossible perfection. I even have customized underwear, but let's not go there.

Replicating the shooting arena (2004, post Athens)

Ivan Lendl had replicated the US Open court in his backyard. Coincidentally, he reached eight straight US Open finals. Homework is never to be underestimated. For shooters, the environment they compete in is crucial, from the solidity of floors to the quality of light. So in my home range, at various times, I had shooting stations made of wood, cement, sport flooring. Or just cement with differing elevations at each station.

At the Beijing World Cup in 2008, which is also a test event prior to the Olympics, I noticed that the panels on which the targets hung were made of dark pine wood. I photographed them and had a similar backdrop created at home. The lighting at Beijing was extreme... I replicated this as well.

I hired a marriage hall for a day (2008)

Players who are unused to Centre Court at Wimbledon can apparently get unsettled not just by its aura but its size. Similarly, the hall for the Olympic final in Beijing was unusually big and I needed to find a sense of myself within it. So I hired a marriage hall for a day in Chandigarh, set up a range in it and practised.

Using an ultrasound to monitor myself (2007)

Stillness is an art. Isolating and activating those muscles, especially in the core, which ensures stability, can be extraordinarily difficult. Then a trainer suggested an ultrasound. During the procedure, while lying on the bed, I could go beyond an imagined mental picture and actually see the muscles as I tried to activate them.

Working on my fitness (2006-'07)

In 2007 I went to a fitness camp in Melbourne and worked with trainer Len Chong. Every day, up to six hours a day, we went at it. Twice a day I ran, 5 kilometres each time. I lifted kettle bells, did Pilates, worked on my lower back. I'd surf the Internet and buy equipment that could help. Most was junk, but it indicated my dislike for the half measure.

If I had to put a number on it, I'd say the gym-work was worth an extra point or two in Beijing. The separation between winning and not winning is infinitesimal and now I knew at least that exhaustion could be fended off, I wouldn't fade. I worked to the point where I believe no one was training like me.

Choosing the correct pellets (2008)

The Chinese shoot well for many reasons. One, I told myself, has to be ammunition. So in practice, I shot ten German pellets at a target. The grouping was 6.5 mm. Then I conducted the test with Chinese pellets. The grouping was 5.4 mm. In my sport, this was the difference between gold and nothing. I phoned a friend in Hong Kong and asked him to order the pellets. Weeks later I had 10,000 rounds.

Every pellet I required was first weighed by me on a sensitive scale. If it was off by a couple of grams, out of the window. Every pellet was then studied under a magnifying glass. If there was a bulge or scratch on the nose, into the dustbin. This has an effect on accuracy. Trust me, I tested for it. When I won gold in Beijing, I used these pellets.

Neuro-feedback to chart my brain and body (2008)

Sports psychologist Tim Harkness told me he wanted to look inside my head. Place sensors on me, hook me to a machine and chart what my brain and body did when I shot well; what conversations I had with myself, how much I sweated, why my skin reached a particular temperature under stress; what emotional control I was capable of. Because in competition it is not just aiming that decides gold, but the capacity to be in sustained command of the emotional self and maintaining a clinical focus.

If it was Athens 2004, I would have refused Tim access. But by Beijing 2008 I had learnt flexibility. If it helps, try it now.

Winning was all I thought about.

So first we enter my lungs and the heart. Sensors are attached to chest and abdomen and we listen into, and calculate, the most basic of human functions. Breathing.

My respiratory rate prior to the Olympics was fourteen to fifteen cycles per minute, but I learn, slow down, slow down, and by the time I get to Beijing it is down to four to five cycles per minute. I need this. I need to be stable, to hold my breath, stay calm.

Then we move to my skin, which tells so many tales. Anxiety is always hovering and its calling card is sweat. The negative thought has a physical response on the skin, and it is so subtle it doesn't always register with me. But it does on the machine. So as I shoot, with sensors attached to my fingertips to measure sweat, I stay focused on a graph on the computer. The calmer I am, the steadier the line.

Every day we slog. Even Tim is taken aback when I shoot eight hours straight till I run out of pellets.

When I shoot well, Tim can see evidence on the screen. My brain is quiet, relaxed, not lit up like a tree at Christmas. It is fascinating, because I have to train both parts of the brain simultaneously, to be aware (motor skills) yet calm (no talking). I have to give my mind and body the best possible opportunity to execute a trained skill. Nothing must affect me, no thoughts must invade my consciousness.

Distraction is inevitable, handling it is crucial. Tim constructs a pulley so that suddenly, in my line of vision, a flag pops up. He shakes rattles as I shoot. He and trainer Heath Mathews stand inches away from me and shout 'miss, miss, miss'. They mock me, tease me, but the harder they sledge, the better I shoot.

Taking a Leap of faith

Because Uwe (Riesterer) had been a commando once, he suggested commando training a week before I left for Beijing. I jumped at it. The only way to handle fear is to confront it.

So I started. I walked a log of wood across a 50-60-foot divide. I walked a Burma Bridge, which is essentially a thick rope bridge that constantly swings. This one was 60 feet high. I clambered up a rock-climbing wall about 42 feet high. And then came the pizza pole, fitted with steel rungs like on some telephone poles. Every rung I climbed, with the wind buffeting me from the nearby sea, the harder it got. The legs freeze, the mind quits. To just put one foot onto a higher rung, to lift, to pull, each step taking me further away from the ground that is our comfort zone, requires an enormous leap of faith. It is a leap of discovery, for it helps you locate physical and mental reserves you weren't sure you owned. Uwe knew, and so did I, that he had pushed me almost to my limit. And it wasn't over yet. Now I had to step off the pole into thin air. Just trust the wires.

For Uwe, this was a perfect lesson, stress managed without

thinking. In the Olympic final, when the last shot is called, you have to just go, you just rely on your skills, you just shoot that 10.5 that is required.

Discovery arrives in the strangest places. On the afternoon of 25 July 2008, I knew I could win gold in Beijing. I knew this while standing alone, at the top of a 40-foot pole in Munich, harassed by the wind and assaulted by fear. I knew because I had taken a leap of faith.

I stepped off the pizza pole and felt serene and victorious.

A week later, I arrived in Beijing without fear. On the day of the final, I thought back to Munich, to the pole, to the moment. I wasn't sure I was going to win. But I knew I had the reserves needed to win because I had reached deep into myself and found them.

A shot at history

My first shot of the final is a 10.7. I laugh inside.

Suddenly, wonderfully, I am in a perfect zone of calm, stability, balance, breathing. This is who I am now, a child of competitive DNA, a product of neuro-feedback and commando training, a confection of practice, experimentation, courage, desire, will, luck.

Every drop of sweat shed, every trick tried, every pellet examined, every technical correction made, all of it has come together.

I picked up my rifle for one last time, looked at the sight, was aiming slightly to the left, corrected myself and pulled the trigger. Just touched it really. It was over fast. A few seconds.

And it was as close to perfect as you can get.

10.8

Gaby (Buhlmann) flashed me a 'thumbs up' for victory, but I misunderstood. I thought she meant a medal. When she hugged me, I was still asking, 'Did I win?' I couldn't see the main scoreboard. Then she said: 'Yes, gold.'

I had won India's first individual Olympic gold with the highest score ever in an Olympic final.

∽

2

I believe one of the reasons we went through such a remarkable growth period was that we had this atmosphere of free discussion. A company will get nowhere if all of the thinking is left to management.

AKIO MORITA

∽

On the afternoon of 7 May 1946, some twenty people gathered on the third floor of a burned-out department store building in war-devastated downtown Tokyo to establish a new company: Tokyo Telecommunications Engineering Corporation. **Akio Morita** helped take this small radio repair shop and turn it into the powerhouse electronics company, the Sony Corporation. Along with co-founder Masaru Ibuka, Morita is responsible for encouraging the amazing growth of the Japanese electronics industry over the years. Morita's business strength was in his ability to study both Western and Eastern cultures and combine the best parts of each.

Morita was a great man manager. According to him, 'We in Japan see the bases of success in business and industry differently. We believe that if you want high efficiency and productivity, a close cordial relationship with your employees, which leads to high morale, is necessary.' He believed that once hired, an employee's school records were a matter of the past, and no longer needed to evaluate his work or promotion. He made it a point to visit every facility of the company, and to try to meet and know every single employee. He believed that the company must not throw money away on huge bonuses for executives or other frivolities but must share its fate with the workers.

The Walkman was the dream child of Morita who wanted to be able to listen to operas during his frequent trans-Pacific plane trips. The invention revolutionized the way people would listen to music by allowing them to carry it along wherever they went.

In these excerpts from Morita's autobiography, *Made in Japan*, we come to know the planning and thought that went behind making the Walkman, and how Sony got its name.

∽

Success Comes from Will-power
Akio Morita

From Sonny Boys to Sony

I had decided during my first trip in 1953 that our full name—Tokyo Kogyo Kabushiki Kaisha—was not a good name to put on a product. It was a tongue-twister. It seemed to me that our company name didn't have a chance of being recognized unless we came up with something ingenious. I also thought that whatever new name we came up with should serve double duty—that is, it should be both our company name and our brand name. That way we would not have to pay double the advertising cost to make both well known.

Ibuka and I took a long time deciding on a name. We agreed we didn't want a symbol. The name would be the symbol, and therefore it should be short, no more than four or five characters. We wanted a new name that could be recognized anywhere in the world, one that could be pronounced the same in any language. Ibuka and I went through dictionaries looking for a bright name, and we came across the Latin word *sonus*, meaning 'sound'. The word itself seemed to have sound in it. Our business was full of sound, so we began to zero in on *sonus*.

At that time in Japan borrowed English slang and nicknames were becoming popular and some people referred to bright young and cute boys as 'sonny'. And we also thought of ourselves as 'sonny-boys' in those days. Unfortunately, the single word 'sonny' would be pronounced 'sohn-nee', which means to lose money. That was not the way to launch a new product. We pondered this problem for a little while and the answer struck me one day: why not just drop one of the letters and make it 'Sony'? That was it!

Fitting it into a pocket

We managed to produce our first transistorized radio in 1955 and our first tiny 'pocketable' transistor radio in 1957. It was the world's smallest, but actually it was bigger than a standard men's shirt pocket, and that gave us a problem for a while, even though we never said which pocket we had in mind when we said 'pocketable'. We came up with a simple solution—we had some shirts made for our salesmen with slightly larger than normal pockets, just big enough to slip the radio into.

Our plan is to lead the public with new products rather than ask them what kind of products they want. So instead of doing a lot of market research, we refine our thinking on a product and its use and try to create a market for it by educating and communicating with the public. Sometimes a product idea strikes me as a natural.

The Walkman example

As an example, I can cite a product surely everybody knows

of—the Walkman. The idea took shape when Ibuka came into my office one day with one of our portable stereo tape recorders and a pair of our standard-size headphones. He looked unhappy and complained about the weight of the system. He explained: 'I like to listen to music, but I don't want to disturb others. I can't sit there by my stereo all day. This is my solution—I take the music with me. But it's too heavy.'

I knew from my own experience at home that young people cannot seem to live without music. Almost everyone has stereo at home and in the car. Ibuka's complaint set me into motion. I ordered our engineers to take one of our reliable small cassette tape recorders we called Pressman, strip out the recording circuit and the speaker, and replace them with a stereo amplifier. I outlined the other details I wanted, which included very lightweight headphones that turned out to be one of the most difficult parts of the Walkman project.

It seemed as though nobody liked the idea. At one of our product planning meetings, one of the engineers said, 'It sounds like a good idea, but will people buy it if it doesn't have recording capability? I don't think so.'

Nobody openly laughed at me, but I didn't seem to be convincing my own project team, although they reluctantly went along. I even dictated the selling price to suit a young person's pocketbook, even before we made the first machine. The Pressman tape recorder was a relatively expensive unit, selling for forty-nine thousand yen in Japan, and I said that I wanted the first models of our new stereo experiment to retail for no more than thirty thousand yen. The accountants protested but I persisted.

I thought we had produced a terrific item, and I was full of enthusiasm for it, but our marketing people were unenthusiastic. They said it wouldn't sell. But I was so confident the product was viable that I said I would take personal responsibility for the project. I never had reason to regret it. The idea took hold and from the very beginning the Walkman was a runaway success. Soon we could hardly keep pace with the demand and had to design new automated machinery to handle the flood of orders.

My point of telling this story is simple. I do not believe that any amount of market research could have told us that the Sony Walkman would be successful, not to say a sensational hit that would spawn many imitators. And yet this small item has literally changed the music-listening habits of millions of people around the world.

It was this kind of innovation that Ibuka had in mind when we wrote a kind of prospectus and philosophical statement for our company in the very beginning: 'If it were possible to establish conditions where persons could become united with a firm spirit of teamwork and exercise to their hearts' desire their technological capacity then such an organization could bring untold pleasure and untold benefits.'

My vision of the future is of an exciting world of superior goods and services, where every nation's stamp of origin is a symbol of quality, and where all are competing for the consumers' hard earned money at fair prices that reflect appropriate rates of exchange. I believe such a world is within our grasp. The challenge is great; success depends only on the strength of our will.

3

If you want to be happy, set a goal that commands your thoughts, liberates your energy, and inspires your hopes.

ANDREW CARNEGIE

∽

Andrew Carnegie's life story is the true rags to riches story. Born in 1835, he started his career at the age of thirteen as a bobbin boy in a cotton factory. Mostly self taught, he moved from being a Western Union messenger boy to a telegraph operator and then to a series of positions leading to the superintendent of the Western Division of the Pennsylvania Railroad. As the American economy expanded in the aftermath of the Civil War, railroads were built across the length and breadth of the country. Carnegie invested in companies manufacturing for the railroads, producing wheel axles, rails and bridges. He expanded his business ventures to encompass the building of bridges, locomotives and rails.

Carnegie was the man who changed charity into philanthropy.

In 'The Gospel of Wealth' he analysed for the purpose of the accumulation and administration of wealth: 'The man of wealth thus becoming the mere trustee and agent for his poorer brethren, bringing to their service his superior wisdom, experience and ability to administer, doing for them better than they would or could do for themselves... The man who dies thus rich, dies disgraced.' These principles were to guide him for the rest of his life as he systematically proceeded to give away over 350 million dollars. His fortune continues to fund education, research, promotion of peace and the general good of society. One of the greatest philanthropists of his era, Carnegie shares his secret to success in this article that appeared in the *Pittsburg Bulletin* on 19 December 1903. Though written over 110 years ago, his advice still holds true, more so today when so many people use any means necessary to attain fame and money. He emphasizes on the importance of being honest to yourself and honest to your work and having good work ethics.

How to Succeed in Life
Andrew Carnegie

Everybody wants to preach to the young, and tell them to be good and they will be happy. I shall not enter far upon that field, but confine myself to presenting from a business man's standpoint of view, a few rules, which, I believe, lie at the root of business success.

First: Never enter a bar-room. Do not drink liquor as a beverage. I will not paint the evil of drunkenness, or the moral crime; but I suggest to you that it is low and common to enter a bar-room, unworthy of any self-respecting man, and sure to fasten upon you a taint which will operate to your disadvantage in life, whether you ever become a drunkard or not.

Second: I wish young men would not use tobacco; not that it is morally wrong, except in so far as it is used in excess and injures health, which the medical faculty declares it does. But the use of tobacco requires young men to withdraw themselves from the society of women to indulge the habit. I think the absence of women from any assembly tends to lower the tone of that assembly. The habit of smoking tends to carry young men into the society of men whom it is not desirable that they should choose as their intimate associates. The practice of chewing tobacco was once common. Now it is considered offensive. I believe the race is soon to take another step forward, and that the coming man is to consider smoking as offensive as chewing was formerly considered. As it is practically abandoned now, so I believe smoking will be.

Third: Having entered upon work, continue in that line of work. Fight it out on that line (except in extreme cases), for it matters little what avenue a young man finds first. Success can be attained in any branch of human labour. There is always room at the top in every pursuit. Concentrate all your thought and energy upon the performance of your duties. Put all your eggs into one basket and then watch that basket, do not scatter your shot. The man who is director in a half dozen railroads and three or four manufacturing companies, or who tries at one and the same time to work a farm, a factory, a line of street cars, a political party and a store, rarely amounts to much. He may be concerned in the management of more than one business enterprise, but they should all be of the one kind, which he understands. The great successes of life are made by concentration.

Fourth: Do not think a man has done his full duty when he has performed the work assigned him. A man will never rise if he does only this. Promotion comes from exceptional work. A man must discover where his employer's interests can be served beyond the range of the special work allotted to him; and whenever he sees his employer's interests suffer, or wherever the latter's interests can be promoted, tell him so. Differ from your employers upon what you think his mistakes. You will never make much of a success if you do not learn the needs and opportunities of your own branch much better than your employer can possibly do. You have been told to 'obey orders if you break owners.' Do no such foolish thing. If your employer starts upon a course which you think will prove injurious, tell him so, protest, give your reasons, and stand to them unless convinced you are wrong. It is the young man who does this, that capital wants for a partner or for a son-in-law.

Fifth: Whatever your wages are, save a little. Live within your means. The heads of stores, farms, banks, lawyers' offices, physicians' offices, insurance companies, mills and factories are not seeking capital; they are seeking brains and business habits. The man who saves a little from his income has given the surest indication of the qualities which every employer is seeking for.

Sixth: Never speculate. Never buy or sell grain or stocks upon a margin. If you have savings, invest them in solid securities, lands or property. The man who gambles upon the exchanges is in the condition of the man who gambles at the gaming table. He rarely, if ever, makes a permanent success. His judgment goes; his faculties are snapped; and his end, as a rule, is nervous prostration after an unworthy and useless life.

Seventh: If you ever enter business for yourself, never endorse for others. It is dishonest. All your resources and all your credit are the sacred property of the men who have trusted you; and until you have surplus cash and owe no man, it is dishonest to give your name as an endorser to others. Give the cash you can spare, if you wish, to help a friend. Your name is too sacred to give.

Do not make riches, but usefulness, your first aim; and let your chief pride be that your daily occupation is in the line of progress and development; that your work, in whatever capacity it may be, is useful work, honestly conducted, and as such ennobling to your life.

To sum up, do not drink, do not smoke, do not endorse, do not speculate. Concentrate, perform more than your prescribed duties; be strictly honest in word and deed. And may all who read these words be just as happy and prosperous and long lived as I wish them all to be. And let this great fact always cheer them: It is impossible for anyone to be cheated out of an honourable career unless he cheats himself.

4

My message, especially to young people, is to have courage to think differently, courage to invent, to travel the unexplored path, courage to discover the impossible and to conquer the problems and succeed. These are great qualities that they must work towards.

A.P.J. ABDUL KALAM

Popularly referred to as the Missile Man of India for his work on the development of ballistic missile and launch vehicle technology, **A.P.J. Abdul Kalam** worked as an aerospace engineer with the Indian Space Research Organisation (ISRO) and the Defence Research and Development Organisation (DRDO) before he became India's eleventh President. He has been perhaps one of the most loved and respected Presidents of India. During his tenure at the top he was much more than a titular head, bonding with the people of the country, especially the youth, as he shared his Vision 2020. Little wonder that most of the younger generation idolize this soft-spoken scientist.

Dr Kalam once famously remarked: 'What is the secret of success? Right decisions. How do you make right decisions? Experience. How do you gain experience? Wrong decisions.'

How true. To succeed you have to fail…before you learn to walk you have to fall a few times. So don't give up if you fall. Pick yourself up, dust away the grime and move forward. There is always a light at the end of the tunnel.

I had the good fortune of interviewing Dr Kalam some months ago. I remember asking him about his latest book, *My Journey* and the message that he wanted to share through it. Dr Kalam replied: 'It does not matter who you are, have a dream, do not allow problems to defeat you, become the captain of the problem, defeat the problem and succeed. As long as you have a dream you have the capacity to not make the problem your captain, you become the captain of the problem.'

I Succeeded Because I Failed
A.P.J. Abdul Kalam

You need to taste failure to aspire for success

In my life, which has been long and eventful, I have seen great heights of success. I have been part of ventures that have contributed to the growth of our nation in the field of science and technology; I have also had the privilege of occupying the highest office in the country. There are many achievements to look back upon—some of my own doing and some where I had the privilege to be part of teams, which were immensely talented. Yet, I firmly believe that unless one has tasted the bitter pill of failure, one cannot aspire enough for success. I have seen both sides of the coin and have learnt life's toughest lessons when I have stared into the pit of despair that failure brings with it. These lessons are well worth recounting and remembering, as they have helped me work my way through many difficult situations.

'This is just not good enough, Kalam'

One of the earliest such episodes from my life happened when I was a student of aeronautics at MIT. My design teacher there was Professor Srinivasan, who was also the head of the institute. Once, we were placed in teams of four students each, and our team had to design a low-level attack aircraft. I was in charge of coming up with the aerodynamic design. We worked very hard for weeks. My teammates were designing all the other components, like the propulsion, structure, control and instrumentation. Since our other course work was over at the time, we spent long hours discussing our ideas and researching them. We were all keen to impress our professors with our project. They kept an eye on the progress and after a few days, Professor Srinivasan asked to see the design I had created. When I showed it to him, he examined it with his characteristic critical eye. I stood by, waiting with bated breath to hear his verdict. I still remember the way his eyebrows crinkled as he looked at the paper spread out in front of him. Then he straightened up and his next words stunned me. 'This is just not good enough, Kalam,' he said. 'I expected much better from you. This is dismal work and I am disappointed that someone with your talent has come up with work like this.'

I stared at the professor, dumbfounded. I had always been the star pupil in any class and had never ever been pulled up by a teacher for anything. This feeling of embarrassment and shame was a new experience for me, and I did not like it one bit. The professor shook his head some more and told me that I had to redo the entire design, starting from scratch and rethinking all my assumptions. I agreed shamefacedly. Then he broke the next bad news. Not only was I supposed to do the work again, I had to finish it in three days! 'Today is Friday afternoon, young man. I want to see a flawless configuration drawing by Monday evening. If you are unable to do so, your scholarship will be stopped.' I was even more dumbfounded now. The scholarship was the only way I could afford to be in college. Without it I would have to stop my studies. My own ambitions, the dreams of my parents, my sister and Jalalluddin flashed before my eyes and seemed to recede to a distance. It was unthinkable that the future could turn so bleak with a few words spoken by my professor.

I was determined to prove myself

I got to work right away, determined to prove myself. I skipped dinner and remained at the drawing board through the night. Where earlier the components of my design were floating in my head, now they suddenly came together and took on forms and shapes I could work with. The concentrated work I put in seemed to brush away all the cobwebs of the mind. By the next morning, I was working like a man possessed. I took a short break to eat and freshen up, and went back to work again.

By Sunday evening, my work was nearly complete—an elegant, neat design that I was proud of. While I was putting my final touches to it, I sensed a presence in the room. It was the professor, still dressed in his tennis whites, on his way back from the club. I didn't know how long he had been standing there, watching me. Now, as our eyes met, he came forward. He looked critically at my work for many minutes. Then he straightened up and smiled. To my amazement, he hugged me affectionately. Then patting me on the back, he said, 'I knew I was putting you under immense pressure when I rejected your work the other day. I set an impossible deadline—yet you have met it with work that I can only call outstanding. As your teacher, I had to push you to your limits so that you could recognize your own true potential.' After two days of extreme dejection, those words were music to my ears and revived my confidence and self-belief.

That day I learnt two lessons: a teacher who has his or her student's progress in mind is the best possible friend, because the teacher knows how to make sure that you excel. And second, there is no such thing as an impossible deadline. I have worked on many tough assignments, some of which had the country's top leaders watching over my work, but the assurance I gained in my capabilities at MIT thanks to Professor Srinivasan, helped me later in life too.

I want to be a pilot

After MIT, I started my working life. Little did I know that even tougher lessons were to follow. I went to work at Hindustan Aeronautics Limited (HAL) in Bangalore. There I learnt a lot about aircraft and their design and technology. By now I was very sure that I wanted a career in flying. When I emerged as a graduate aeronautical engineer from HAL, I got two job opportunities. One was in the air force and another at the Directorate of Technical Development and Production (DTD&P [Air]) at the Ministry of Defence. I received interview calls from both. The first was in Dehra Dun and the second in Delhi. I set forth with great hope in my heart.

My first close sight of an aircraft had been at MIT, where two decommissioned aircraft were kept for the demonstration of various subsystems to the students. They had held a special fascination for me, and I was drawn to them again and again. They represented for me man's ability to think beyond his boundaries, and to give wings to dreams. I had chosen aeronautical engineering as my area of study because of my fascination for flying. Over the years I had nurtured the hope to be able to fly; to handle a machine as it rose higher and higher in the stratosphere was my dearest dream.

As I made my way from Madras to north India for the interviews, I played this dream over and over again in my mind. I was finally on the threshold of becoming a pilot! The journey from Tamil Nadu to Dehra Dun was a long one—not just geographically but also in terms of the distance I would travel from my humble origins to the prize that lay in the foothills of the Himalayas—a place in the air force as a pilot.

Working on my communication skills

I first halted in Delhi for my interview. I was confident and the interview was an easy one, not requiring me to push the boundaries of my knowledge too far. I spent a week in Delhi and then proceeded to Dehra Dun for my interview at the Air Force Selection Board. Here, I should mention that at the time, as a young man in my early twenties, I was just beginning to understand how to conduct myself in the wider world. When I had first moved from Rameswaram to the bigger cities for my studies, I was a shy, tongue-tied boy. I had to work hard to develop some assertiveness in my personality. I did this by trying to communicate with different people from all kinds of backgrounds. It was not easy and there were many moments of frustration and disappointment. However, by the time I finished my studies and headed out to look for a job, my personality was better developed and I was able to articulate my thoughts well enough in English and Tamil.

I failed to become an air force pilot

To return to my interview at the Air Force Selection Board, as I started answering the queries put forth to me, I realized that along with qualifications and engineering knowledge, they were also looking for a certain kind of 'smartness' in the candidate. Physical fitness and an articulate manner were what they were seeking. I gave it my best. I had wanted this job for so long and so deeply that I was determined yet anxious, confident and at the same time tense. Finally the results were announced. I had stood ninth in a batch of twenty-five. There were only eight places available. I had failed to realize my dream of becoming an air force pilot.

Dealing with my failure

I still remember the ache in my heart as I attempted to make sense of what had happened. When a dearly held desire begins to break up, one can feel nothing but despair and emptiness as one tries to come to terms with the end of a dream. I could not bear to be indoors after seeing the result. I had to go out for air and be in the open, because all around me the walls seemed to close in. I walked around for a while till I reached the edge of a cliff. I stood there looking down at the shimmering waters of a lake and wondered what I should do next. Plans needed to be changed and priorities reassessed. I decided to go to Rishikesh for a few days and seek a new way forward.

I reached Rishikesh the next morning. I took a dip in the Ganga—a river I had heard so much about, but was seeing and experiencing for the first time in my life. I had been told about the Sivananda Ashram that was located a little way up a hill. I walked there. As I entered I felt a strange vibration, a sense of tranquility that was like a balm for my restless soul. Sadhus were seated all around, deep in meditation. I hoped that one among them would be able to answer the questions that troubled me and soothe my worries. I was granted an audience with Swami Sivananda himself. My being a Muslim did not affect him in any way. Instead, before I could speak, he asked what had filled me with sorrow. I only fleetingly wondered how he knew about my sadness before I embarked on an explanation of the recent developments in my life. He listened calmly and then washed away my anxieties with a smile of deep peacefulness. His next words were some of the most profound I had ever heard. His feeble yet deep voice still resonates when I think of them:

'Accept your destiny and go ahead with your life. You are not destined to become an air force pilot. What you are destined to become is not revealed now but it is predetermined. Forget this failure, as it was essential to lead you to your destined path. Search, instead, for the true purpose of your existence… Surrender yourself to the wish of God.'

I was convinced God had a larger plan for me

That lesson made a deep impression on my mind. Truly, why fight against destiny? This failure, I was sure, was part of a larger plan that God had for me. I ruminated long about this as I went back to Delhi. There, I found that I had been accepted as senior scientific assistant at DTD&P. I gave up my dream of making a career out of flying. I understood now that there was plenty of other work to be done, and I was going to put my heart and soul into the job that had been given to me.

In this way I started my working life. Like me, I am sure almost every person who sets out with a goal has had to face unexpected obstacles. We've had to rethink our goals, reorient our paths. Each setback teaches us a new facet of life and something about our own personalities. When we tackle obstacles, we find hidden reserves of courage and resilience we did not know we had. And it is only when we are faced with failure do we realize that these resources were always there within us. We only need to find them and move on with our lives.

A life in science: three lessons

If I am asked now as to what were the biggest lessons I learnt in the development of the SLV, I will say there are three aspects.

Lesson 1: The role of science in development

There was the first revelation to me about the role of science and technology, research and engineering in the development of a country. In the number of teams that were working on the SLV there were scientists, researchers and engineers. Who did what and where—as a team leader, I was meant to draw lines and give direction. I learnt that science is open-ended and exploratory. That it sets out to find answers like a traveller goes on a voyage. It is, in fact, a voyage into all that is possible and all that will one day be explained and made possible. Science is a joy and passion. Development, on the other hand, is a closed loop. It takes the work done by scientists and moves it a few steps further. It does not allow for mistakes and exploration. In fact, it uses mistakes for making modifications and upgradations. So where the scientists showed us the way and opened up possibilities that enabled us to build an indigenously designed and developed launch vehicle, the engineers kept us on the path of results, given the time and resources we had on hand. For a project of this nature to succeed, it needed all these parts to work in tandem and in sync, like the pieces of an orchestra.

Lesson 2: Science needs commitment

The second lesson that came to me was about the nature of commitment. In those years, while I myself thought of little else other than the project, there were many others like me who put in tremendous amounts of hard work and passion into it. Yet, more valuable words of wisdom on this were never said to me than those by Wernher von Braun. A giant in the field of rocketry, von Braun had developed the V-2 missiles that destroyed London during World War II. Later, he was inducted into NASA's rocketry programme, where he created the Jupiter missile that was the first missile with a high range. He was a scientist, designer, engineer, administrator and a technology manager. He was, indeed, the father of modern rocketry. I had the privilege of flying with him when he visited India, when I received him at Chennai and escorted him to Thumba. His words to me about the whole nature of our work are still ingrained in my mind. 'You should always remember that we don't just build on successes, we also build on failures.' On the inevitable hard work and dedication required by those in our profession he said, 'Hard work is not enough in rocketry. It is not a sport where mere hard work can fetch you honours. Here, not only do you have to have a goal, but you also need strategies to achieve it as fast as possible.

'Total commitment is not just hard work, it is total involvement. It is also about setting a goal. It is having a goal in front of you that makes a difference to the final outcome of your hard work.' And these words, that I believe I did follow: 'Do not make rocketry your profession, your livelihood—make it your religion, your mission.'

At that time in life I put everything other than the SLV project on hold. I also learnt to manage stress. It is the way your mind handles the difficulties that are strewn in the path of your goal that determines the result. I truly believe we need these difficulties in order to enjoy the final success of any mission.

Lesson 3: Dealing with setbacks

And this leads on to my third lesson from the SLV project—the ability to deal with setbacks and learn from them. It is now well known that the first experimental flight trial of the SLV-3 ended in disaster—the vehicle plunged into the sea. Stage 1 performed perfectly. It was at the second stage that things went out of control. The flight was terminated after 317 seconds and the vehicle's remains, including the fourth stage with the payload, splashed into the sea, 560 kilometres off Sriharikota.

I was numbed beyond belief at the turn of events. Yes, I had experienced failures and setbacks earlier, but this, coming at the end of years of back-breaking hard work, was difficult to absorb. I had no answers as the thought kept racing round and round in my head—'What went wrong?' I was at the end of my physical capabilities as I had been putting up with enormous stress and now, when all of it had come to nought, there was nothing I could say to myself or to those around me that made any sense.

Finally, all I could think of was sleep. I had to sleep, I told myself, before I could go any further on this path of analysis. I remember I must have slept for many hours, and was awoken gently by Dr Brahm Prakash. He was then my boss, but at the time he came to me only as an elder, with concern. He woke me up and made me accompany him to the mess for a meal. We ate together and all the time he gave me solace by not uttering a single word about the launch. The analysis and the rebuilding of the mission would come later. At that moment in time we were just two men, tired beyond belief, yet knowing that what we had created would not come to waste. We knew we had more mountains to climb and higher peaks to conquer in the days to come, but right then he took me under his wings and did what a parent would do to a child after he has lost that coveted race—give him food, let him rest and let him think where the next step lies.

The value of humanity

And that was perhaps the most important lesson I learnt from SLV-3. That humaneness, generosity and understanding can never let you down. At the end of the day, when goals have been set and mapped, when the path has been traversed and obstacles met head on, it is only the values of humanity that will bring true succour. To be able to be gentle and forgiving, compassionate and kind are finally all we need to be in times to come, whether we develop missiles or teach in a school; whether we hold high offices or are parents bringing up children in this confusing world of ours.

5

If people are not laughing at your goals, your goals are too small.

AZIM PREMJI

∽

Following the death of his father, a young **Azim Premji** returned home from Stanford University, where he was studying engineering, to take charge of Wipro in 1967. Wipro, which was then called Western Indian Vegetable Products, dealt in hydrogenated oil manufacturing at the time. Recognizing the importance of the emerging IT sector, Premji took advantage of the vacuum left behind following the exit of IBM from India, and started manufacturing minicomputers. Today, the Chairman of Wipro, with an estimated wealth of more than $12 billion, is, according to Forbes, the third-richest Indian. Over the past forty years he has made Wipro one of the leaders in the software industry in India.

According to Premji, 'Life has many challenges. You win some and lose some. You must enjoy winning. But do not let it go to the head. The moment it does, you are already on your way to failure. And if you do encounter failure along the way, treat it as an equally natural phenomenon. The important thing is, when you lose, do not lose the lesson.'

When it comes to philanthropy, Indians may not be in the same league as Warren Buffet or Bill Gates but Azim Premji stands tall as the 'most generous Indian' with over Rs 8,000 crore worth of donations in 2013. In fact, he is the first Indian to sign up for Giving Pledge, a campaign led by Buffett and Gates, to encourage the wealthiest people to make a commitment to give most of their wealth to philanthropic causes.

In this speech delivered at the Indian Institute of Technology, Madras in 2001, Premji shared with the outgoing class ten lessons that he had learnt in his life.

Perseverance Can Make Miracles Happen

Aʒim Premji

I am a little wary about giving you advice, because advice is one thing young people all over the world do not like receiving. I cannot fault you for that. The world does look very different when it is seen with your eyes. You are filled with enthusiasm and are straining at the leash to get on with life.

And the world is very different from what it was when I was at your age. Never before has the role of technology been so pervasive and so central. The Internet has breached all physical borders and connected the world together like no other force has done before.

For the first time, opportunities for creating wealth in India are at par with the best in world. There is no need for you to sacrifice the joy of remaining in your own country any more.

All opportunities are accompanied by their own challenges. I thought I would share with you a few of the lessons I have learnt in my own life, while leading the transformation at Wipro from a small company three and a half decades back into a global corporation listed on the New York Stock Exchange. I hope you find them useful.

Dare to dream

When I entered Wipro at the age of twenty-one, it was a sudden and unexpected event. I had no warning of what lay ahead of me and I was caught completely unprepared. All I had with me was a dream, a dream of building a great organization. It compensated for my inexperience and, I guess, also prevented me from being overwhelmed by the enormity of the task before me. What I am happy about is that we never stopped dreaming, even when we achieved a position of leadership in every business we operated in India. We now have a dream of becoming one of the top 10 global IT service companies.

Many people wonder whether having unrealistic dreams is foolish. My reply to that is dreams by themselves can never be realistic or safe. If they were, they would not be dreams. I do agree that one must have strategies to execute dreams. And, of course, one must slog to transform dreams into reality. But dreams come first.

What saddens me most is to see young, bright people getting completely disillusioned by a few initial setbacks and slowly turning cynical and some of them want to migrate to America in the hope that this is the solution. It requires courage to keep dreaming. And that is when dreams are most needed—not when everything is going right, but when just about everything is going wrong.

Define what you stand for

While success is important, it can become enduring only if it is built on a strong foundation of values.

Define what you stand for as early as possible and do not compromise with it for any reason. Nobody can enjoy the fruits of success if you have to argue with your own conscience. In Wipro, we defined our beliefs long before it became a fashion to do so. It not only helped us in becoming more resilient to stand up to crises we faced along the way, but it also helped us in attracting the right kind of people.

Eventually, we realized that our values made eminent business sense. Values help in clarifying what everyone should do or not do in any business situation. It saves enormous time and effort because each issue does not have to be individually debated at length. But remember that values are meaningful only if you practice them. People may listen to what you say but they will believe what you do. Values are a matter of trust. They must be reflected in each one of your actions. Trust takes a long time to build but can be lost quickly by just one inconsistent act.

Never lose your zest and curiosity

All the available knowledge in the world is accelerating at a phenomenal rate. The whole world's codified knowledge base (all documented information in library books and electronic files) doubled every thirty years in the early 20th century.

By the 1970s, the world's knowledge base doubled every seven years. Information researchers predict that by the year 2010, the world's codified knowledge will double every eleven hours. Remaining on top of what you need to know will become one of the greatest challenges for you. The natural zest and curiosity for learning is one of the greatest drivers for keeping updated on knowledge. A child's curiosity is insatiable because every new object is a thing of wonder and mystery. The same zest is needed to keep learning new things. I personally spend at least ten hours every week on reading. If I do not do that, I find myself quickly outdated.

Always strive for excellence

There is a tremendous difference between being good and being excellent in whatever you do. In the world of tomorrow, just being good is not good enough. One of the greatest advantages of globalization is that it has brought in completely different standards. Being the best in the country is not enough; one has to be the best in the world. Excellence is a moving target. One has to constantly raise the bar.

In the knowledge-based industries, India has the unique advantage of being a quality leader. Just like Japan was able to win in the overseas market with its quality leadership in automobile manufacturing, India has been able to do the same in information technology.

At Wipro, we treat quality as the number 1 priority. This enabled us not only to become the world's first SEI CMM Level 5 software services company but also a leader in Six Sigma approach to quality in India. However, even today I am dissatisfied with several things, which we are not doing right in the area of customer satisfaction. Doing something excellently has its own intrinsic joy, which I think is the greatest benefit of Quality.

Build self-confidence

Self-confidence comes from a positive attitude even in adverse situations. Self-confident people assume responsibility for their mistakes and share credit with their team members. They are able to distinguish between what is in their control and what is not. They do not waste their energies on events that are outside their control and hence they can take setbacks in their stride. Remember, no one can make you feel inferior without your consent.

Learn to work in teams

The challenges ahead are so complex that no individual will be able to face them alone. While most of our education is focused on individual strength, teaming with others is equally important. You cannot fire a missile from a canoe. Unless you build a strong network of people with complementary skills, you will be restricted by your own limitations. Globalization has brought in people of different origins, different upbringing and different cultures together. Ability to become an integral part of a cross-cultural team will be a must for your success.

Take care of yourself

The stress that a young person faces today while beginning his or her career is the same as the last generation faced at the time of retirement. I have myself found that my job has become enormously more complex over the last two or three years. Along with mental alertness, physical fitness will also assume a great importance in your life. You must develop your own mechanism for dealing with stress. I have found that a daily jog for me goes a long way in releasing the pressure and building up energy. You will need lots of energy to deal with the challenges. Unless you take care of yourself there is no way you can take care of others.

Persevere however hopeless it seems

Finally, no matter what you decide to do in your life, you must persevere. Keep at it and you will succeed, no matter how hopeless it seems at times. In the last three and half decades, we have gone through many difficult times. But we have found that if we remain true to what we believe in, we can surmount every difficulty that comes in the way.

I remember reading this very touching story on perseverance. An eight-year-old child heard her parents talking about her little brother. All she knew was that he was very sick and they had no money left. They were moving to a smaller house because they could not afford to stay in the present house after paying the doctor's bills. Only a very costly surgery could save him now and there was no one to loan them the money. When she heard Daddy say to her tearful mother with whispered desperation, 'Only a miracle can save him now', the child went to her bedroom and pulled a glass jar from its hiding place in the closet. She poured all the change out on the floor and counted it carefully. Clutching the precious jar tightly, she slipped out the back door and made her way six blocks to the local drug store. She took a quarter from her jar and placed it on the glass counter. 'And what do you want?' asked the pharmacist.

'It's for my little brother,' the girl answered back. 'He's really, really sick and I want to buy a miracle. My Daddy says only a miracle can save him. So how much does a miracle cost?'

'We don't sell miracles here, child. I'm sorry,' the pharmacist said, smiling sadly at the little girl.

In the shop was a well-dressed customer. He stooped down and asked the little girl, 'What kind of a miracle does your brother need?'

'I don't know,' she replied with her eyes welling up. 'He's really sick and Mommy says he needs an operation.'

'How much do you have?' asked the man.

'One dollar and eleven cents,' she answered barely audibly.

'Well, what a coincidence,' smiled the man. 'A dollar and eleven cents—the exact price of a miracle for little brothers. Take me to where you live. I want to see your brother and meet your parents. Let's see if I have the kind of miracle you need.'

That well-dressed man was Dr Carlton Armstrong, a surgeon specializing in neurosurgery. The operation was completed without charge and it wasn't long before Andrew was home again and doing well. 'That surgery,' her mom whispered, 'was a real miracle. I wonder how much it would have cost?' The little girl smiled. She knew exactly how much the miracle cost …one dollar and eleven cents…plus the faith of a little child.

Perseverance can make miracles happen.

Have a broader social vision

For decades we have been waiting for someone who will help

us in 'priming the pump' of the economy. The government was the logical choice for doing it, but it was strapped for resources. Other countries were willing to give us loans and aids but there was a limit to this. In the millennium of the mind, knowledge-based industries like information technology are in a unique position to earn wealth from outside. While earning is important, we must have mechanisms by which we use it for the larger good of our society. Through the Azim Premji Foundation, we have targeted over the next twelve months to enroll over a million children who are out of school due to economic or social reasons. I personally believe that the greatest gift one can give to others is the gift of education. We who have been so fortunate to receive this gift know how valuable it is.

Never let success go to your head

No matter what we achieve, it is important to remember that we owe this success to many factors and people outside us. This will not only help us in keeping our sense of modesty and humility intact but also help us to retain our sense of proportion and balance. The moment we allow success to build a feeling of arrogance, we become vulnerable to making bad judgments.

Let me illustrate this with another story.

A lady in a faded dress and her husband, dressed in a threadbare suit, walked in without an appointment into the office of the president of the most prestigious educational institution in America. The secretary frowned at them and said, 'He will be busy all day.' 'We will wait,' said the couple quietly. The secretary ignored them for hours hoping they will go away. But they did not. Finally, the secretary decided to disturb the president, hoping they would go away quickly once they met him.

The president took one look at the faded dresses and glared sternly at them. The lady said, 'Our son studied here and he was very happy. A year ago, he was killed in an accident. My husband and I would like to erect a memorial for him on the campus.' The president was not touched. He was shocked. 'Madam, we cannot put up a statue for every student of ours who died. This place would look like a cemetery.'

'Oh, no,' the lady explained quickly, 'We don't want to erect a statue. We thought we would give a building to you.'

'A building?' exclaimed the president, looking at their worn out clothes. 'Do you have any idea how much a building costs? Our buildings cost close to ten million dollars!'

The lady looked at her husband. 'If that is what it costs to start a university, why don't we start our own?' Her husband nodded. Mr and Mrs Leland Stanford walked away, travelling to Palo Alto, California, where they established the university as a memorial to their son, bearing their name—Stanford University. The story goes that this is how Stanford University began.

6

If I am given a choice I would like to treat only poor patients. But unfortunately the economic reality does not allow me to do that.

DEVI PRASAD SHETTY

No one exemplifies 'a doctor with a heart' better than heart surgeon and philanthropist, **Devi Prasad Shetty**. A strong advocate of affordable healthcare in our country, he is the founder of Narayana Hrudayalaya, the world's largest and cheapest heart care institute.

Dr Shetty was only in class five when he decided that he wanted to become a heart surgeon. After completing his training in general surgery from Kasturba Medical College, Mangalore, he went to Guy's Hospital in the United Kingdom to become a cardiac surgeon. He returned to India in 1989. In 1992, he performed the first successful neonatal heart surgery in the country on a nine-day-old baby named Ronnie. He also operated on Mother Teresa and served as her personal physician. With the help of contributions from his father-in-law, he started the Manipal Heart Foundation at Manipal Hospital in Bangalore. Till date Dr Shetty has performed approximately 15,000 heart operations and has saved thousands of lives. His hospitals make use of economies of scale and perform heart surgeries for one-tenth a cost of what it takes in United States. His insurance scheme, called Yashasvini, which is the cheapest health insurance scheme in the world, covers 4 million people in Karnataka.

Greatly influenced by Mother Teresa, Dr Shetty possesses all the skills and values that a great doctor should have.

How to be the Greatest Doctor
Dr Devi Shetty

The world belongs to the back benchers

This is the way every classroom in the world works. There are people sitting in the back bench of every school thinking that it is the outstanding doctors, outstanding students, who are going to conquer the world. We the average students, the failures, do not play a major role in this world. But interestingly, the world doesn't work like that. The world belongs to the back benchers. There are several studies done across the world which show that outstanding institutions in the world are created by very average and below average students and they build the institution, which is managed by average students. The toppers of these schools work for these two categories of people. I'm not saying that if you are a topper, you can't make it in life. Success is guaranteed for you, but never write off the back benchers because they are the people who change the rules of the game.

Dare to dream big

Always dare to dream big. Dreams are most needed not when everything is going right, but dreams are important when just about everything is going wrong. Remember, in life you can only succeed 50 per cent of the time, you have to fail 50 per cent of the time. There is no one on this earth who has succeeded in everything he has done, so you can't be an exception.

Never never give up

During the Second World War, Nazis were attacking Britain and their allied forces everywhere. The British forces were being thrashed, there was not even a single building left in London which was not bombed by the Nazis. Victory was evident for the Nazis, but Winston Churchill ensured victory for the allied forces. After their success the media wanted to know how he, in that difficult situation, steered the allied forces to success. They invited him to an auditorium; the world's media was watching, and Winston Churchill was asked to give his opinion. He got up, went to the dais, looked at everyone and said only one sentence: 'Never, never, never give up'. So in life you may have many, many problems, you can't be an exception. But never, never give up.

Have a nice attitude

Have a nice attitude, be compassionate. In our organization, like any other organization, we hire people for their attitude… skill can be taught. Many years ago, an old couple was driving towards New York at night, it was snowing heavily, the road was jammed. The couple decided to spend the night in a motel. They entered a motel and the manager politely told them that there were no rooms available, so the old man started pleading, saying

I'm old, I can't drive, my wife is not well, can you accommodate us just for tonight. The manager obliged, the couple spent the night in a warm room, they were happy. The next morning when the old man got up, he went to check out. He found the manager sleeping on a couch in the corridor. He realized then that the manager had given them his room to spend the night. The old man thanked the manager and left. Life went back to normal. A few days later the manager of the hotel received an envelope, with an appointment letter to become the chief executive officer of a hotel called Waldorf Astoria, the most expensive hotel in the world at the time. A manager of a motel became the CEO of the world's most expensive hotel. What was his qualification? Just compassion, good attitude… so develop a good attitude and you will conquer the world.

Failure is temporary

We teach our children to succeed but the world doesn't teach people to cope with failure. When we don't teach people how to cope with failure, when failure happens, we are not geared up for it—we don't know how to cope. When the examination results come out for the tenth standard or eleventh standard, next day in the paper we hear some young student has committed suicide. Suicide is the final solution to a temporary problem. Every problem in this world is temporary; every problem in this world can be overcome. Failure is a part of life.

Do you know who is the safest surgeon? The safest surgeon is one who doesn't operate. When you operate, somebody is going to get hurt, somebody is going to die, but that doesn't prevent you from operating. A ship is safest in the docks but it is not designed to be in the docks. It has to be in the deep sea and face all the problems in the sea. This is how your life is.

Remember in life there is always a second chance. One opportunity closes, hundreds of them open on the way. Remember all failures are temporary.

Learn from others' mistakes

Always learn from others' mistakes. As a surgeon, I wanted to go all over the world to watch other surgeons operate. From a lot of surgeons I learnt how to operate and also from a lot of surgeons I learnt how not to operate. Because when they finish a heart surgery, the heart looks like a dog's leftover dinner. I would not like some of them to even cut my hair. In life when things are going wrong, remember things are never as bad as they look, and when things are looking great, things are never as great as they look. It is always something in between… in life there are no extremes.

Learn from a dragonfly

I want you to learn from a dragonfly. The dragonfly gets attracted to the light. In a bedroom, a light is shining through the glass windows. One window is open, the other window is shut. The dragonfly hits the glass in its attempt to reach the light. It will keep hitting the glass without realizing that all it has to do is to move six inches to the side where the window is open so it can go to the light. It doesn't do that, it will keep on hitting the glass until it gets tired and falls. This is the story of most doctors who want to get into PGC. You want to be a surgeon, never be fixated about the rules, always be fixated about the destination. It doesn't matter how you reach. When one door doesn't open there are many other doors; always explore. When I was a young surgeon in England, my colleague taught me one lesson, he said, 'The only jobs you don't get are the ones you don't apply for.' Keep applying, keep trying, one day you will get where you want to reach.

Be humble

Be humble, be polite, it doesn't cost you anything to be nice to others. As doctors, people touch our feet, they think we are God. They make us feel that we're not ordinary, but remember we are like anybody else. Ultimately what matters in life is how nice you are to others, especially when society wants to put you on a pedestal. You cannot oblige everyone, but you can at least talk to people obligingly, and this is extremely, extremely important for a doctor.

Be spiritual

Be spiritual, I'm not saying you should be religious, it is up to you. But believe in God. As a surgeon I operate on many patients everyday. In heart surgery we take them nearly to death and bring them back. If there is any surgeon in this world who says I will guarantee success, he is kidding. Whatever I do the outcome is never in my hand, it is decided by someone on top. Believe in God, put your best effort and whatever happens it is His decision. And it will always turn out to be good for you.

You are a trustee

God did not create everyone alike, God created people with different sets of skills. If God created everyone alike, who is going to drive my ambulance, who is going to clean the toilets in my hospital? God gave different sets of wisdom to different types of people but with the belief that when he gave me the wisdom to create an institution he also gave me the responsibility to look after the people. That is the difference. The wealth we have created, it is not my wealth, the wealth belongs to the society, I am a trustee and it is my responsibility to look after them. This is what you all have to learn.

Never criticize others

One day one of you will become a very famous surgeon, the best in your city. A patient comes to you who was operated by another surgeon in the city and the patient is not happy with the outcome. What do you do? Do you say that the surgeon did a bad job? Never criticize him. You will never become great by criticizing others. If you say that the surgeon had done a bad job, fine, believe me that message will always reach him and think about the situation: Five years down the line, a patient, your own patient, is upset with you and he goes to the medical council and files a case against you and the medical council creates a committee to enquire and that surgeon is the chairman of the committee. What is he going to do? So never criticize others. Never underestimate the importance of human beings, God has given the power of creation to very, very few people. But he has given the power of destruction to everyone. So nobody is so small that they can't hurt you.

Accept the world as it is

Accept the world as it is and not as it should be. We work in organizations we don't like, we live in a country which we hate, we live in a city where nothing moves. So we make ourselves miserable. Let's come to the personal life. We always feel, if only our spouse were better, if only our children could do better, if only I had a better job. I have a very simple attitude towards my life. I have a perfect relationship with my wife. Do you know the secret? One day, many years ago I told her that you're not okay, I'm not okay. That's okay. Never look at perfection. God never designed this world to be a perfect world.

Mother Teresa and her influence on me

I spent a lot of time with Mother in the last five years of her life. She taught me a lot of values. This is what I want all of you to remember. You may spend a whole life trying to help human beings. But do not expect human beings to reciprocate the way you want them to, they have their own way of reciprocating.

'People are often unreasonable, illogical and self-centred'… you wouldn't have thought Mother could have said that about people, she did say that. But then her statement is 'forgive them anyway'.

'If you are kind, people may accuse you of selfish ulterior motives, be kind anyway.'

'If you are successful you may win some false friends and

some true enemies, succeed anyway.'

'If you are honest and frank, people may cheat you, be honest and frank anyway.'

'What you spend years building, someone could destroy it overnight, but build anyway.'

'If you find serenity and happiness, others may be jealous, be happy anyway.'

'The good you do today, people will forget tomorrow, but do good anyway.'

'Give the world the best you have got and it may never be enough, but give the world the best you've got anyway.'

Now I want you to look at the last sentence: 'In the final analysis it is between you and God, it never was between you and them, anyway.'

Ultimately it has nothing to do with your patient or society. It is between you and God. Everything else has no meaning.

Did you call your mother to say you love her?

I just want to ask you a question. How many of you have called your mother in the last month and told her that you love her? I want an honest answer. You know, in our country grown-up children do not want to hug their parents and parents do not hug their children and we never tell our parents that we love them. There are parents who never tell their children that they love them but that doesn't mean that they do not love them. They always feel, both parties feel, that the other party knows. Interestingly, the other party doesn't know. So it is very important that any occasion you get, just call or just tell them that you are grateful to them, you love them. We all feel that we are grateful to our parents, one day we will become very successful, and very great. And we'll go to your parents and tell them how grateful we are and how much we love them. But sadly when we reach there, they may not be there.

Who is your customer?

Now as you are graduating, your parents, your friends and everyone are going to advise you on how to set up your shop, how to practice and how to treat rich people because they have the money and they can pay you well for your services. But I would like to tell you that rich people can run faster than you. Never try to build your practice based on rich people. It is a matter of time, rich people have no choice, they have to come to you but if you go after them, they will run faster than you.

The secret to success is caring for the poor because they are the ones who will sing your song, they are the ones who follow you wherever you go. When I used to work in Kolkata, I treated a large number of poor patients from Bangladesh. Some years ago there was a survey conducted in Bangladesh on who is the most popular person among Bangladeshis. You must be thinking they chose some film star or politician. No, they voted me. And I've been to Bangladesh only twice.

There is a beautiful picture I took in front of my house. It is of a person called a 'kuwar carpenter'. When the sewage pipe gets choked where rich people like us live, he has to get into the sewage pipe and clear the blockage, so that people like us, our life is protected. To get into the pipe he has to get drunk.

He dies due to cirrhosis of the liver; if cirrhosis spares him, he will die due to leptospirosis. And when he is sick he has to stand in the long queue in front of the government hospitals and no one cares. There are nine thousand of them in the city of Bangalore so you can imagine how many of them are there in the whole country. They are the people who look after our lives. Can't we do something about it? The day you think you have a responsibility towards him, you will become the greatest doctor on earth.

∽

7

Let your passion for your work carry you through all the setbacks they can throw at you. Be it wind, water, resignations, scandals, whatever—you can prevail. Your insurance for overcoming these perils is free—it's called never giving up!

DONALD TRUMP

∽

Donald Trump is the very definition of the American success story. He has continually set new standards of excellence while expanding his interests nationally and internationally as chairman and president of The Trump Organization and the founder of Trump Entertainment Resorts. It's said often that the road to success comes through hard work, determination and personal sacrifice. Trump is one such example.

Throughout his business career, Trump has seen astonishing highs and lows. He is one man who knows all about turning defeat to victory. Today his name is synonymous with some of the biggest and most prestigious real estates in the US. Early in his career he learned that every building project faces unexpected delays and obstacles. He began to prepare for adversity and even welcomed it. In Trump's own words: 'I believe the so-called "impossible" is actually very possible if you're willing to work very hard, and if you realize that problems can become opportunities.'

The star of the hit reality TV series *The Apprentice*, Donald Trump is also a best-selling author having written a number of 'business classics'.

Never Give Up

Donald Trump

I had such an amazing reversal of fortune in the early 1990s that I am listed in the *Guinness Book of World Records* for the biggest financial turnaround in history. I don't recommend anyone aim for the same goal, but when you've been on the financial high wire, it gives you a certain perspective that might be helpful to other people.

I don't think anyone gets away with a challenge-free experience. My situation in the early 1990s wasn't looking good. I had billions in loans I couldn't pay, and I had personally guaranteed 975 million of that debt. I could easily have gone bankrupt. That was a tremendous low. The banks were after me. People avoided me. There was a recession, and the real estate market was almost nonexistent.

The lowest point

Then in March of 1991, both the *Wall Street Journal* and the *New York Times* ran front page stories (on the same day!) detailing my predicament and the total financial ruin that would happen any moment. The loss of my empire was big news across the world. They were sure I was finished. It would have made a fantastic story—except that it was happening to me.

That was the lowest moment I had encountered in my life. Even the phones in my office were quiet, which had never happened before. In fact, I suddenly had a lot of quiet time to think, and I reviewed the situation objectively. It became clear to me that part of what got me into this situation was that I had lost my perspective and started to believe the news stories about me having 'the Midas touch' when it came to business.

The turning point

However, giving up is something that never entered my mind. Not for one second, and that's one reason I think I confounded my critics. They were trying to skewer me, but it had the opposite effect—it just made me want to make a comeback and in a big way.

What gave me this fortitude? I'm not sure, but being tossed aside as a 'has-been' or a 'wash-up' by the world press might have had something to do with it. I began to see my situation, believe it or not, as a great opportunity.

Then there was the turning point, and that turning point was my attitude. My accountants still remember the night they were in the conference room until all hours in the woe-is-us mode, and I suddenly walked in to tell them about all the new projects I had lined up for us. I was in an exuberant mood, and my descriptions were colourful and optimistic. They thought I had cracked, but I had reached a point where I knew it was time to move forward. It wasn't an act I put on—I was ready.

Focus on the solution, not the problem

As it turns out, that was indeed the turning point. All of us decided to focus on the solution and not on the problem–right then. That's an important lesson: Focus on the solution, not the problem.

Failure is not permanent

It's odd, but in retrospect, I think having a near wipeout made me a better businessman and certainly a better entrepreneur. I really had to think in out-of-the-box ways to keep from being buried alive. I also relied on something I'd like to discuss here: positive thinking. Believe me, it works. It got me where I am today—which is far richer and more successful than I was before the reversal started for me in the 1990s.

A lot of success depends on how well you can handle pressure. It may seem like a hard fact of life, and it is, but there is something you can do about it. Envision yourself as victorious. Focus on that instead of nagging doubts and fears. Focus on objective insights and solutions. Pressure can diminish and disappear when you clobber it with a positive attitude. Even if you don't feel indomitable, act that way for a while. It helps!

I feel strongly about the importance of wholeness. It's a combination of all the components of life that make us healthy, happy, and productive. To my mind, the opposite of wholeness is failure. If it happens, and sometimes it does, the best remedy is to move forward, to realize that failure is not permanent, and to immediately focus in the right direction. Ultimately, a solution will show up.

I've seen some people get completely swallowed up by failure. The worst thing you can do to yourself is to believe that bad luck is your due. It isn't! It's not just intelligence or luck that gets us places, it's tenacity in the face of adversity.

Go with your gut instinct

I often tell people that I listen to everyone, but the decision will ultimately be mine. That's a good way to be in life and in business. Listen to others, but never negate your own instincts. Not one single person, except Mark Burnett and NBC, was enthusiastic about *The Apprentice* and my participation in it. All my advisors thought it was a risk, that it would bomb, that my credibility as a businessman would be jeopardized, that my focus would be lost, and that I was making a huge and ultimately very public mistake. When I look back, it's pretty amazing how dead set against it they were. My gut instinct told me it was the right thing to do, without consulting anybody.

The week before *The Apprentice* aired for the first time, in January 2004, I remember wondering if that would be the last week of my well-respected life. What got me through was remembering my gut instinct that said, 'This is a great idea—go for it!' Fortunately, the show was a sensation. If I hadn't decided to take the risk, go against my advisors, and do the show, none of this would have happened. One side effect is that my brand became far better known around the whole world, and there was an amazing media interest in everything I did. That's another form of free advertising. So when I advise you to take risks, there's a reason for it.

Top 10 List for Success

1. Never give up! Do not settle for remaining in your comfort zone. Remaining complacent is a good way to get nowhere.
2. Be passionate! If you love what you're doing, it will never seem like work.
3. Be focused! Ask yourself: What should I be thinking about right now? Shut out interference. In this age of multitasking, this is a valuable technique to acquire.
4. Keep your momentum! Listen, apply and move forward. Do not procrastinate.
5. See yourself as victorious! This will focus you in the right direction.
6. Be tenacious! Being stubborn can work wonders.
7. Be lucky! The old saying, 'The harder I work, the luckier I get' is absolutely right on.
8. Believe in yourself! If you don't, no one else will either. Think of yourself as a one-man army.
9. Ask yourself: What am I pretending not to see? There may be some great opportunities right around you, even if things aren't looking so great. Great adversity can turn into great victory.
10. Look at the solution, not the problem. And never give up! Never, never, never give up. This thought deserves to be said (and remembered and applied) many times. It's that important. Good luck!

8

Age is just a number. When I started, I never worried about how long I was going to play. I had very specific goals, and that's what I really chased.

LEANDER PAES

⌒

In the age of 24/7 media and Facebook likes, the word 'legend' is used all too easily. But for **Leander Paes**, legend sounds right. Consider this: he has won his Grand Slam titles over three decades. If that hasn't impressed you enough, try this: his singles record against both Pete Sampras and Roger Federer is one win each and no loss! But my old friend is more than records and surly statistics. There is so much more to this lad (lad?! the man is forty!) who played his early tennis at Kolkata clubs DI and CC&FC before his father Vece did what most parents wouldn't do—packed him off to the Britannia Amritraj Tennis Academy in Chennai to pursue his passion.

With fourteen Grand Slam men's doubles and mixed doubles titles under his belt, Paes is without a doubt one of the greatest doubles players the tennis world has ever witnessed. Exuding extreme confidence and a never-say-die attitude on court, he bears many a scar of great battles fought and many a Davis Cup match won. Notwithstanding all his Grand Slam wins and considerable achievements, he has always remained the boy next door. Whether it's paying a visit to the hole-in-the-wall Bengal Hair Dressing Salon next to Mithai in Beckbagan or charming septuagenarian 'uncles' and 'aunties' in the clubs of Kolkata he grew up in or playing a practical joke on his eldest sister Jackie… Leander is, just Leander.

∽

My Passion Keeps Me Going

Leander Paes

I am an Olympic baby

If you go by genetic engineering, I am an Olympic baby. As some of you may know, both my parents were athletes. My mom captained India in basketball, all five feet nothing of her. My mom is the reason I got my speed, she was lightning quick both on her feet and with her mind, very clear in her thoughts. My father played hockey for India in 1972 at the Munich Olympic Games, the only Olympics to be shut down for four days, because of terrorism. Out of every tough story a good thing comes through, at least I believe so—I was conceived in those four days. Makes me wonder what my parents were really training for. Dad went on after that to achieve a bronze medal, which he reckons was his biggest achievement. I reckon his biggest achievement was conceiving me during those four days.

Dad's dream

I was born in June 1973, and before I was born my dad would go out and talk about how his first son is going to be a professional athlete and the first number one athlete India has ever seen. Dad worked really hard with me, since I was about the age of three. I still remember being in a crib with all these multi-coloured balls around me and I had to reach up and get them, I didn't realize I was doing abs... Dad made it a fun game.

Even today when I bring home a trophy, my father is the last one to greet me, but I must say he is the first one for me when I lose a match or when I have something not so good happen in my life. Mom on the other hand reckons everything I do is fantastic. So I have to be a little careful.

Football, my first love

Since I was a little boy, Dad introduced me to every single sport. I played for school in cricket, hockey, soccer, boxing, athletics; I represented school in swimming as well. There was no tennis at that point of time. I thought tennis was an older man's game. At that age when I was about eight or nine years old, football was my first love. If I have a football in front of me or any object circular in shape, I guarantee you it would not touch the floor for fifteen minutes.

At the age of twelve I was selected for a junior soccer programme in Europe. Soccer being my first love, I used to sleep with my soccer boots. I used to wake up in the morning, polish them and go for training in them. But when I was asked to move to Europe to play for another country and to play for something that was more of a team sport, a club sport rather than for an individual, or a country or a flag, I gave up my dream of being a soccer player.

From football to tennis

It wasn't an easy choice for a twelve year old because at that age all you want to do is have fun, at that age you have no guarantees as to where life is going to go. And when I gave up that dream, my dad asked me, what's next? I said, tennis. I can assure you that I had no idea what I was talking about at that time. And I said to Dad, 'Find me the best tennis academy on the planet and give me a year, in one year I will tell you whether I can do it or not.'

The first year alone was hard

My first year was hard; my parents separated the day I left for the tennis academy. I lived in Chennai for a year, as the youngest boy among eight. I was struggling to win games on the sets let alone matches. My first year I got beaten pretty bad. My roommate, who was the second youngest on the team, was two years older than I was, and he was a great confidant, a great team mate. Rohit spent many nights with me, basically telling me how I could learn the skills of tennis. He was a very talented tennis player and as much as Rohit told me I could learn the skills of it, I one day told him that we will probably play together. We ended up playing for India together, it was great fun. But it took me five years to really learn how to control a yellow fuzzy ball and how to make it dance to your rhythm.

On tour as a junior

Tennis is a tough sport in India, this was especially so back in the mid 1980s. The infrastructure, the knowhow, the knowledge of fitness, the knowledge of diet, the knowledge of sports medicine was not really there, but my father, being a doctor as well as an athlete, was a big advantage I had. Using Dad's and Mom's knowledge of sport, five years later I became No. 1 in the world, in the juniors. And as much as my journey began five years before, the real journey started when I was eighteen.

Early years on the professional circuit

While I was playing the juniors, I had the international tennis federation look after some expenses of travel, my coaches, my tournament schedules, my doubles partners, my practice coach. But the minute I finished the junior circuit and I turned professional and came into the big bad world of professional sport, I found myself very alone. I found myself in a small town in Wolfsburg, Germany. I had about $30 in my pocket and a train ticket and my racket bag. I did not have money to get my next train or flight from Wolfsburg to Garmish up in the mountains in Germany, where the first Winter Olympics happened.

It's a cold and lonely day when you don't win

I did not have any money in my pocket for a hotel room, and that night late in October 1991, I spent in the locker room of Wolfsburg tennis club. The locker attendant was a sixty eight year-old man, about 300 pounds, beautiful smile, soft eyes who didn't speak a word of English. I didn't speak a word of German at that time, and I had to find a way to communicate to him that I needed to spend a night in the locker room because I didn't have money for a hotel room. It was in the middle of winter, so it was not like you could find a train station or a hotel lobby, but I managed to communicate with him by buying him a cup of coffee and just sitting and interacting with him using eye contact, using human touch… and before I could ask him he had four towels for me. I still remember they were green in colour, one was to use as a little blanket, one was to lay down on the floor, one was to roll up as a pillow and the fourth one was for a shower the next morning. He told me in his broken English that he was going to lock the tennis centre because of security but he left one window open on court number 5, and if there was an emergency then I had to jump out of that window. I was not jumping nowhere, I was staying right in, it was the height of winter at that time. But the next morning I made sure I woke up before any of my comrades or teammates showed up at the site. I was the only Indian at the tournament; I was the only Indian pretty much for a decade playing on the professional tour, after Ramesh Krishnan.

I won two matches that day, one singles and one doubles, I won two matches the next day. I won two on Saturday and two on Sunday and I won the singles and the doubles and till today I remember the night in Wolfsburg locker room. It was pretty cold that night and even today with thirty-one Grand Slam finals and an Olympic medal and representing you for twenty-four years, I will never ever forget late October of 1991 Wolfsburg, because it's a cold and lonely day when you don't win.

The moral of the story

What's the moral of the story? Many things. The moral of the story is that we Indians can be world beaters. But with the discipline and the hard work we have as students of life, we Indians make great students. We respect our elders, we listen to them, we sift what they say to see what matters to us and we try to incorporate in our lives what we learn from our teachers, be it in the classroom or be it on the tennis court or be it in a computer science room. No matter what walk of life we are in we have to then incorporate and execute what we learn from our adults, from our parents. The single thing that I am most proud of is to have proven that a young Indian boy from Kolkata with not much opportunity can be a world leader.

Special thanks to my team

Surrounding yourself with a good team, surrounding yourself with good quality people—their skills don't have to match—their passion and their enthusiasm for excellence need to match, is important. You get people from different skill sets that bring to the table their specialty in their way, but at the end of the day it's up to each and every one of you to set a vehicle of communication, to set a methodology of understanding what they are trying to say. When you really ask them the right questions and really understand, what they are saying to you, then you need to break that down and do it in your style. I wouldn't be where I am today without my team and that's why I honour them whenever I have a chance.

I am an optimist-realist

I am extremely confident—some even say bordering on cockiness. That is so untrue; I'm not cocky at all. I would describe myself as an optimist-realist. I'm aware of my shortcomings and I'm always learning new ways to overcome them. I believe every action in life has a karma attached to it and we live out that karma. Everything else is hard work, discipline and practice. I have very, very fastidious work ethics.

My energy during matches is not rehearsed at all. It is confidence and karma. For people on my team, my confidence is almost like raw, infectious energy that charges them. On the other hand, for my opponents, my confidence confuses them; my almost in-your-face body language puts them off. They call me brash and many other names but I'm not a bit brash. I have to live with it; this is my karma.

To me winning is all about being in rhythm or form. You win or lose all the time. Confidence is not that superficial—it's innate. Some people may show it. Some are silent like Sampras, Edberg or Borg; just go near them and you can feel their confidence.

What keeps me going

What keeps me going: I think my passion for life. I think I haven't yet satisfied the hunger that I have to master the game of tennis. So if you're talking tennis itself, I'm 5'10", thanks to Mum. I don't have a big serve, but my team and I keep trying to get enough explosiveness in my legs, because I've inherited that speed and explosion from Mum as well, to get enough explosiveness off the floor of a tennis court and to be able to have a big serve. Speed is usually something which diminishes with age, but there is certain methodology that you can use whether it is computers, whether it is using agility on a floor, whether it is using modern training methods for eye-hand coordination, for eye-feet coordination—at the end of the day it's all between your two temples. If the synergy between your body and mind and your soul is intact and you work on that every single day there is no reason why you can't be the best physically.

The world knows Leander's backhand top spin is his weakest shot. I could get round it by turning it into my forehand topspin. Sometimes, when I couldn't do that in the 80s as the game was much slower I resorted to a chip. Now, with physically stronger athletes entering the court, chip is not an option. So the day I learn to hit a good topspin backhand and I can do ten in a row I might think of retiring.

My greatest motivation

My achievements in the Olympics as well as in the Davis Cup have given me the greatest joys of my life. Yes I've beaten Sampras, yes I've contested thirty Grand Slam finals, but none of them compares to the thrill of playing for the country. Conversation at the dining table at breakfast or dinner was always about being the best we can be. It's no wonder that I get motivated more for playing for the country, playing for the flag and playing for my people than I do when it comes to playing for dollars or myself or trophies. People keep asking me: Explain this, when you say you're playing at Wimbledon you say it's the greatest arena you have stepped in; you say that the inner court at Wimbledon is the Mecca of tennis. But when you play Davis Cup, whether you play at the NSCI or the DLTA stadium, Delhi, whether you play in Frejus in the south of France against a formidable French team that has four top 10s in the world, how do you find it in you to invariably come out on top?

When I was younger I didn't have the answer, because sometimes you do what you just do. You don't always have to find an answer or a reason, you just do it, but as the years have gone by I have tried to break it down and my humble explanation is, if you really deeply desire to achieve something, no matter what it is, if that burning desire is so strong, you will make sure you surround yourself with the right team, the right people and you will ask the right question to find the solution to be the best you can be.

Playing for your country, playing for your flag, playing for your people is the greatest high and it is probably the single largest driving factor that has enabled me to play for twenty-four years. But when you really break it down, the passion to achieve excellence as lonely—as that road is—you got to make it a happy road. You got to find tricks and sometimes trick your mind a little bit by getting to know yourself really well to just set a spark off. Once you set off that spark to achieve excellence, the rest of your skill sets kick in and then it becomes a rhythm.

The one governing theory that I've lived my life with is if you can handle triumph and disasters and treat both these two impostors just the same then let's play the game of life, and play it hard.

9

I don't study cricket too much. Whatever I have learned or experienced is through cricket I've played on the field, and whatever little I have watched.

MAHENDRA SINGH DHONI

⁂

Mahi, Captain Cool, MS… whatever you may call him, **Mahendra Singh Dhoni** is without a doubt India's most successful captain ever. He is the only player to have captained his country to victory in the ICC World Cup, ICC WorldTwenty20 and the Champions Trophy. He has also led his IPL team, Chennai Super Kings, to two victories, and India to No. 1 ranking in Tests. In the past people have labelled him a fluke, a lucky captain, someone in the right place at the right time, but over and over again Dhoni has proven that he is an astute leader with a cool temperament and a good attitude. When he started off as captain he had to deal with many bigger names and stars on the Indian team, which he managed extremely well. He extracted the best out of these stars at most times without ruffling feathers. But perhaps his greatest asset is his ability to stay calm, on the pitch with India staring at defeat or out in the real world where detractors are willing to write him off after a team debacle. Dhoni's leadership skills are a lesson for all young managers in managing extremely stressful work environments without losing their composure.

∽

Cricket, the Mind Game
Mahendra Singh Dhoni

Preparing the body and the mind

In cricket, the mind is very important. There are many players with talent and good technique who never get the success they deserve. Some players with good technical skills sometimes do well for a while but then fail to carry on or perform consistently. I believe the missing ingredient is mental control. Though the mind is the determining factor, you still have to be fit and have good technique. If you rate fitness on a scale of one to ten, you might feel you should get your level to seven or eight to perform well. You don't have to be at ten. But if you make circles around the pillars of fitness, technique, strategy and mental skills, the circles would overlap each other, so you have to be good at all of them.

When you prepare yourself for a game, you can't just prepare your body, you must also prepare the mind in order to get 100 per cent out of yourself in the game. Both physical and mental components are vital but the mind is more important.

Cricket has changed over the years and is now a very demanding game. Mental and physical preparation is critical today. For instance, you can't just turn up for training and decide not to dive at the ball during the practice session. At training you must consistently practice everything that you do in a match. You must do them everyday and at every session to improve and maintain your skills. The mind then helps you to transfer the things you do at practice to the game.

I was very competitive

During my teenage years, I used to play several different sports and although I was not good at all of them I was nevertheless very competitive. When I played I wanted to win and I was very determined to win. But I knew that if I was just playing a game and if I lost, it wasn't the end of the world or the end of my life.

I constantly tried to give 100 per cent to whatever I was doing. I also realized that my opponents might be more talented and better prepared than I was, so I never left any stone unturned if I thought it would help me to win. That will to win was strengthened by my love and passion for sports.

I play best under pressure

I love the challenge and the pressure. They have always pushed me to do well. People say a lot of negative things about pressure. Pressure to me is just added responsibility. That is how I look at it. It's not pressure when God gives you an opportunity to be a hero for your team and country. Sometimes you get disappointed after a bad or a tough game. It is natural to feel let down after a bad performance but you should always learn something from your experience and your failure. You should identify the positives of your game and the lessons you learned and then use them to improve your planning, preparation and performance in the next game. You should also watch the other players to see the things they do well and spot the mistakes they make and the things that restrict them.

Playing for the country is important but you also need a steady income

Every player should regard the journey to success as an exciting and challenging learning experience. Even for the very talented players, performance is a learning process that takes time, effort and persistence. If you are motivated to learn you will learn, something new everyday.

Playing for your country should be your main motivating force. But today you need to have a good income and livelihood. Only a few players have a professional education or academic qualifications.

A good cricketer has seven to ten years to earn the money that will sustain him for life after cricket. So he must balance his love for the country with a good income and livelihood. Of course, love and passion for the game and the need for recognition are other powerful motivators. But, in today's competitive and fast-changing world we cannot ignore the importance of money in the life of a cricketer.

My advice to upcoming players

First and foremost, love and enjoy your sport. If you do not enjoy it you will not learn to play the game as quickly or as well as you should.

Second, keep things simple. The more you complicate the process the harder it will be for you to improve your game. For example, when you tell yourself to watch the ball and play it on its merits, you might have other thoughts like scoring runs or not getting out on your mind. Those thoughts can break your concentration and prevent you from watching the ball. If you know that the bowler can bowl an out-swinger, an in-swinger and a good bouncer as well, you have three other things to think about. But the more you think about what the bowler might do, the more complex and difficult batting becomes.

Third, capitalize on your strengths, improve on your weaknesses, and recognize your limitations.

It is very important to realize at the right time what you are good at, whether you're good at cricket or any other sport or at studies. If you are good at studies and you want to play cricket, you may work harder than any other person but you may not achieve it. So it's something you have to balance in life, and be practical where you are good and then channelize your efforts in the right direction to be successful in life.

I try to be positive always

When I go to Australia or South Africa I try to be positive and see the visit as a challenge and an opportunity to explore, learn and improve my game. I try not to be negative or worry about the pace and bounce of the wickets or the things that could possibly go wrong.

Learning and improvement take time. When you leave nursery school you don't expect to go straight into a graduate school. In the following years you slowly improve as a student and when you reach a certain standard you graduate and afterwards go on to higher levels. The same thing happens in sport.

You should therefore be patient and persistent and you should keep things simple and enjoy your sport. Not only should you enjoy your own performance on the field but you should also get pleasure from sharing your experiences with other players and from creating an atmosphere that helps the guy sitting next to you in the dressing room to perform better.

You need to have a strong foundation

God gives natural gifts to all of us. We need to realize that and work to strengthen them and to improve in those areas where our weaknesses lie. Mastering the basics is a key to good performance. When a skyscraper is being built, a lot of time and money is spent on constructing the foundation under the ground. In sport, investment in the foundation is also extremely important. The basics are the foundation on which performance is built. If that foundation is weak, performance will fall apart under pressure and intense competition. A strong foundation improves confidence, concentration and performance.

Handling pressure

At the 2012 World Cup, I still remember playing the Australia quarter-final and people saying that was the biggest game at the World Cup. Then it was Pakistan in the semi-final. I remember travelling and people were like, 'Win this game and we don't care about the finals.' As soon as we won the semi-final, it was like, 'You have to win this because it doesn't matter what you've done. If you don't win the final it won't be really nice.' So there was a lot of pressure, which was the ultimate thing.

I don't practice yoga or meditation. I love to be in the moment, I love to analyse things a bit. Very often what is important is to realize what went wrong, not only when you are losing a series or a game, but also when you are winning a series; when you need to realize what are the areas you need to work on.

Winning the World Cup

It was one of the biggest things for us as Indian cricketers. We are playing at the top level. We all want to be part of a World Cup-winning side. The last time we won the proper fifty-over version was twenty-eight years back. So most of the people in the side wanted to win the World Cup, and as soon as we got into a position where we saw the World Cup coming into our dressing room, emotions started to flow. If you see, before the post-match presentation, almost every player cried. I cried too. It's very difficult to control an emotion like that. I was controlling myself. I wanted to quickly go up to the dressing room, and I saw two of my players crying and running to me. All of a sudden, I started crying, and I looked up and there was a huddle around me. Each and everyone cried.

I was not born a leader

I was very a shy kid, and the first time I captained was very late in my career. Very late means I was playing maybe Under-19 or something like that. And I never had a fair amount of exposure when it came to leadership.

I felt it's always important not to think whom you are leading. More important is what needs to be done, and to channelize the kind of resources you have to accomplish the target, to be successful at what you are supposed to achieve.

Importance of self-confidence

I was always confident of my ability. I knew I was going to play for my country. It was only a matter of time.

Self-confidence has always been one of my good qualities. I am always very confident. It is in my nature to be confident, to be aggressive. And it applies in my batting as well as wicketkeeping. It doesn't matter to me personally what people are saying so long as I am doing well with the gloves and am confident about my ability as a wicketkeeper. Maybe because I bat aggressively and go for big hits at times, people tend to remember my batting.

So, am I a wicketkeeper-batsman or a batsman-wicketkeeper? When India is fielding, I am a wicketkeeper-batsman; when India is batting, I am a batsman-wicketkeeper! But, seriously, both are my main jobs. I have to specialize in both of them. I can't afford to be less than 100 per cent in any of the two roles. I think they complement each other and give me my identity.

Living in the moment

I love being in the present. When I was playing for my school, the only thing I wanted to do was get selected for the Under-16 or the Under-19 district teams. When I was selected for the district I would think about the next level, which was getting selected for the state side. I'm a person who lives very in the moment. Frankly, I never thought that I would represent my country one day. Now I'm leading my country, so it's like a fairytale. I never thought I'd do all these things. I lived in the moment, I kept working hard. I never expected to get a call for the Indian cricket team in the very next meeting.

If you don't really have a dream, you can't really push yourself, you don't really know what the target is. I think it is very important to stay focused, have short-term goals, not look too much in the future, and try to win each and every series that is coming. Of course, you won't be able to do that. But it is important that you prepare yourself in that way and try to give your best on the field.

10

Performance leads to recognition. Recognition brings respect. Respect enhances power. Humility and grace in one's moments of power enhances the dignity of an organization.

N.R. NARAYANA MURTHY

∾

In 1981, **N.R. Narayana Murthy**, along with six others, founded Infosys, which is new a global leader in consulting, technology and outsourcing solutions. It started with a small investment of ₹10,000, which he borrowed from his wife, Sudha Murty. Under his leadership, Infosys was listed on NASDAQ in 1999. Murthy articulated, designed and implemented the Global Delivery Model, which has become the foundation for the huge success in IT services outsourcing from India. He has led key corporate governance initiatives in India. He is an IT advisor to several Asian countries.

Time magazine refers to him as the Father of the Indian IT sector; *Fortune* magazine has him listed as one of the twelve greatest entrepreneurs of our time; The Asian Awards recognized him as Philanthropist of the Year and he was voted NDTV's Icon of the Year in 2011. These are just some of the accolades and recognitions bestowed on the co-founder of Infosys.

But what is the secret to his success? Narayana Murthy

advocates his success to five mantras which he follows: Be open to learn and take ideas from others; by using data to arrive at the best decision, adopt the best ideas and implement them; work faster because the faster you work, the more ideas and better innovation you will bring to the table; implement these great ideas with a higher level of excellence today than yesterday. If you follow these steps diligently, there is no reason why you will not succeed.

10 Life Lessons
N.R. Narayana Murthy

After some thought, I have decided to share with you some of my life lessons. I learned these lessons in the context of my early career struggles, a life lived under the influence of sometimes unplanned events which were the crucibles that tempered my character and reshaped my future.

I would like first to share some of these key life events with you, in the hope that these may help you understand my struggles and how chance events and unplanned encounters with influential persons shaped my life and career.

Later, I will share the deeper life lessons that I have learned. My sincere hope is that this sharing will help you see your own trials and tribulations for the hidden blessings they can be.

Chance events can sometimes open new doors

The first event occurred when I was a graduate student in control theory at IIT, Kanpur, in India. At breakfast on a bright Sunday morning in 1968, I had a chance encounter with a famous computer scientist on sabbatical from a well-known US university.

He was discussing exciting new developments in the field

of computer science with a large group of students and how such developments would alter our future. He was articulate, passionate and quite convincing. I was hooked. I went straight from breakfast to the library, read four or five papers he had suggested, and left the library determined to study computer science.

Friends, when I look back today at that pivotal meeting, I marvel at how one role model can alter for the better the future of a young student. This experience taught me that valuable advice can sometimes come from an unexpected source, and chance events can sometimes open new doors.

From confused Leftist to a determined, compassionate capitalist

The next event that left an indelible mark on me occurred in 1974. The location: Nis, a border town between former Yugoslavia, now Serbia, and Bulgaria. I was hitchhiking from Paris back to Mysore, India, my home town.

By the time a kind driver dropped me at Nis railway station at 9 p.m. on a Saturday night, the restaurant was closed. So was the bank the next morning, and I could not eat because I had no local money. I slept on the railway platform until 8.30 p.m. in the night when the Sofia Express pulled in.

The only passengers in my compartment were a girl and a boy. I struck a conversation in French with the young girl. She talked about the travails of living in an iron curtain country, until we were roughly interrupted by some policemen who, I later gathered, were summoned by the young man who thought we were criticizing the Communist government of Bulgaria.

The girl was led away; my backpack and sleeping bag were confiscated. I was dragged along the platform into a small 8x8 foot room with a cold stone floor and a hole in one corner by way of toilet facilities. I was held in that bitterly cold room without food or water for over seventy-two hours.

I had lost all hope of ever seeing the outside world again, when the door opened. I was again dragged out unceremoniously, locked up in the guard's compartment on a departing freight train and told that I would be released twenty hours later upon reaching Istanbul. The guard's final words still ring in my ears: 'You are from a friendly country called India and that is why we are letting you go!'

The journey to Istanbul was lonely, and I was starving. This long, lonely, cold journey forced me to deeply rethink my convictions about Communism. Early on a dark Thursday morning, after being hungry for 108 hours, I was purged of any last vestiges of affinity for the Left.

I concluded that entrepreneurship, resulting in large-scale job creation, was the only viable mechanism for eradicating poverty in societies.

Deep in my heart, I always thank the Bulgarian guards for transforming me from a confused Leftist into a determined, compassionate capitalist! Inevitably, this sequence of events led to the eventual founding of Infosys in 1981.

While these first two events were rather fortuitous, the next two, both concerning the Infosys journey, were more planned and profoundly influenced my career trajectory.

Do we sell Infosys?

On a chilly Saturday morning in winter 1990, five of the seven founders of Infosys met in our small office in a leafy Bangalore suburb. The decision at hand was the possible sale of Infosys for the enticing sum of $1 million. After nine years of toil in the then business-unfriendly India, we were quite happy at the prospect of at least seeing some money.

I let my younger colleagues talk about their future plans. Discussions about the travails of our journey thus far and our future challenges went on for about four hours. I had not yet spoken a word.

Finally, it was my turn. I spoke about our journey from a small Mumbai apartment in 1981 that had been beset with many challenges, but also of how I believed we were at the darkest hour before the dawn. I then took an audacious step. If they were all bent upon selling the company, I said, I would buy out all my colleagues, though I did not have a cent in my pocket.

There was a stunned silence in the room. My colleagues wondered aloud about my foolhardiness. But I remained silent. However, after an hour of my arguments, my colleagues changed their minds to my way of thinking. I urged them that if we wanted to create a great company, we should be optimistic and confident. They have more than lived up to their promise of that day.

In the seventeen years since that day, Infosys has grown to revenues in excess of $3 billion, a net income of more than $800 million and a market capitalization of more than $28 billion,

28,000 times richer than the offer of $1 million on that day.

In the process, Infosys has created more than 70,000 well-paying jobs, 2,000-plus dollar millionaires and 20,000-plus rupee millionaires.

A final story

On a hot summer morning in 1995, a Fortune 10 corporation had sequestered all their Indian software vendors, including Infosys, in different rooms at the Taj Residency hotel in Bangalore so that the vendors could not communicate with one another. This customer's propensity for tough negotiations was well known. Our team was very nervous.

First of all, with revenues of only around $5 million, we were minnows compared to the customer.

Second, this customer contributed fully 25 per cent of our revenues. The loss of this business would potentially devastate our recently-listed company.

Third, the customer's negotiation style was very aggressive. The customer team would go from room to room, get the best terms out of each vendor and then pit one vendor against the other. This went on for several rounds. Our various arguments why a fair price—one that allowed us to invest in good people, R&D, infrastructure, technology and training—was actually in their interest failed to cut any ice with the customer.

By 5 p.m. on the last day, we had to make a decision right on the spot whether to accept the customer's terms or to walk out.

All eyes were on me as I mulled over the decision. I closed

my eyes and reflected upon our journey until then. Through many a tough call, we had always thought about the long-term interests of Infosys. I communicated clearly to the customer team that we could not accept their terms, since it could well lead us to letting them down later. But I promised a smooth, professional transition to a vendor of the customer's choice.

This was a turning point for Infosys.

Subsequently, we created a Risk Mitigation Council which ensured that we would never again depend too much on any one client, technology, country, application area or key employee. The crisis was a blessing in disguise. Today, Infosys has a sound de-risking strategy that has stabilized its revenues and profits.

I want to share with you, next, the life lessons these events have taught me.

Learning from experience

I will begin with the importance of learning from experience. It is less important, I believe, where you start. It is more important how and what you learn. If the quality of the learning is high, the development gradient is steep, then, given time, you can find yourself in a previously unattainable place. I believe the Infosys story is living proof of this.

Learning from experience, however, can be complicated. It can be much more difficult to learn from success than from failure. If we fail, we think carefully about the precise cause. Success can indiscriminately reinforce all our prior actions.

Power of chance events

A second theme concerns the power of chance events. As I think across a wide variety of settings in my life, I am struck by the incredible role played by the interplay of chance events with intentional choices. While the turning points themselves are indeed often fortuitous, how we respond to them is anything but so. It is this very quality of how we respond systematically to chance events that is crucial.

Your mindset

Of course, the mindset one works with is also quite critical. A fixed mindset creates a tendency to avoid challenges, to ignore useful negative feedback and leads such people to plateau early and not achieve their full potential. A growth mindset leads to a tendency to embrace challenges, to learn from criticism and such people reach ever higher levels of achievement.

Self-knowledge

The fourth theme is a cornerstone of the Indian spiritual tradition: self-knowledge. Indeed, the highest form of knowledge, it is said, is self-knowledge. I believe this greater awareness and knowledge of oneself is what ultimately helps develop a more grounded belief in oneself, courage, determination, and, above all, humility, all qualities which enable one to wear one's success with dignity and grace.

Based on my life experiences, I can assert that it is this belief in learning from experience, a growth mindset, the power of chance events, and self-reflection that have helped me grow to the present.

Back in the 1960s, the odds of my being in front of you today would have been zero. Yet here I stand before you! With every successive step, the odds kept changing in my favour, and it is these life lessons that made all the difference.

I hope you believe that the future will be shaped by several turning points with great learning opportunities. In fact, this is the path I have walked to much advantage.

A final word

When, one day, you have made your mark on the world, remember that, in the ultimate analysis, we are all mere temporary custodians of the wealth we generate, whether it be financial, intellectual or emotional. The best use of all your wealth is to share it with those less fortunate.

I believe that we have all at some time eaten the fruit from trees that we did not plant. In the fullness of time, when it is our turn to give, it behooves us in turn to plant gardens that we may never eat the fruit of, which will largely benefit generations to come. I believe this is our sacred responsibility, one that I hope you will shoulder in time.

∽

11

Nothing is impossible. I have made many things possible. The amount of hard work which I put in my game is really important. Motivation comes from winning and that is what keeps me going.

SAINA NEHWAL

Saina Nehwal is arguably one of India's greatest sportswoman ever and without a doubt India's greatest women's badminton player. At just twenty-three she has achieved so much: she is the first Indian to win an Olympic medal in badminton, she is the first Indian to win the World Junior Badminton Championships and also the first Indian to win a Super Series tournament.

Nehwal's story is the perfect example of what one needs to give up and what one needs to work on to become successful. While her friends and classmates were studying, watching movies and growing up like 'normal' teenagers, she was hard at work from four in the morning till eight at night, perfecting her strokes on court. While her classmates were attempting to pass their Board exams, she was already conquering the world, winning one career title after another. Her story is also about how important it is for a young champion to have a supporting family who is there by her side through all the ups and downs.

It's All About Hard Work
Saina Nehwal

Two lucky strokes that changed my life

Papa heard of a badminton summer camp being organized. He decided to enroll me there. Both Mummy and Papa had played badminton at Hisar, with Mummy having played for Haryana state as well. They loved the game and that's probably why this camp caught Papa's eye. To Papa's dismay, we were told that selections for the camp were over. Papa would not take no for an answer and looking back, I must thank God for that! He was determined to get me into the camp, and requested the coaches to give me a chance and see my game. Surprisingly, the coaches agreed and I went on court. I had played a little badminton earlier but at that time, to me it was just another game. That morning I think I was plain lucky because my first stroke was a lovely smash! Both Nani sir (P.S.S. Nani Prasad) and Goverdhan (S.L. Goverdhan Reddy) were impressed and the next thing I knew, I had a place in the summer camp.

For the one month that followed, I went to badminton camp every morning. I had never attended a summer camp before and now I had to do exercises like 400-metre run, skipping, running up and down stairs, cross-country racing of some 4-5 kilometres… I was working out for the first time in my life and it took me quite a while to get used to it. Mummy decided that training in the mornings was not enough. So every afternoon, we would practice at home. She would teach me the game, the strokes and tell me what I should focus on at camp the next day.

When the camp ended, we were told that one player amongst us would be selected for further training. I reached the finals but lost to Deethi, a player from Maharashtra. She was selected for training. Unfortunately for her, she could not stay as she had to return home to Nagpur, which meant that the spot was open for me, and I slipped right into it. Two lucky strokes in one summer, and they changed my life!

Mummy saw the potential in me

Until this point I had not thought beyond the holidays. I am not sure whether my parents had either, although Mummy is the ambitious one in the family. She decided that since I had the potential to be a good badminton player, I should continue. She was the one who pushed me to stay with the training and the daily discipline of practice.

Hours put in to become a champion

Every morning, Papa and I would wake up at four, get ready and take the bus to the stadium. I trained between six and eight, and then we would rush back so that I could make it to school on time. Most days I barely reached in time for the morning assembly. In the afternoons, Mummy would meet me at the school gates at 3.30 and take me to the stadium. Papa would pick us up later, and by the time we reached home it would be nine in the night and I'd be exhausted. I am sure Papa was equally tired too, but neither he nor Mummy expressed it in front of me.

During the first few years, this rigorous training was extremely hard to keep up. I was also growing, and my leg muscles would ache constantly. Many nights, I used to wake up crying in pain, and Mummy would come to my room immediately and massage my legs with almond oil so that I could train the next day. I remember having dark circles under my eyes too, but giving up was somehow never an option. I had fallen in love with the game. I liked to play it, liked to be on court, and liked winning a game very much.

All of this did not mean that academics were not important. In fact, right from the beginning, my ambition was to be a doctor, never a 'world-class badminton player'. But now, with my badminton training schedule, things started changing. Although Mummy and Papa made sure I never fell behind on schoolwork, I didn't have much time left for studying when I came home after practice. I was also too tired to sit up and do homework.

Did my parents put too much pressure on me?

I am often asked if my parents put too much pressure on me. I've thought about it quite a lot, and my answer is no, they didn't. They saw that I showed a lot of interest in the game and was willing to work hard, and they encouraged it. The rigour of training and hard work was not just on me, it was on them as well. They too woke up early and followed up on my training. They also kept up with the demands of the training with me. But for that kind of dedication and commitment, there's no way I could have reached where I have. There are some things in life you just can't do alone. And this happens to be one of them.

My first big win

That same year, 1999, I participated in the Under-10 district-level tournament held in Tirupati. I won the tournament, my first big win. With it also came my first earnings, Rs 500 in prize money. What did I do with the money? I gave it to my parents, as I still do with my winnings.

From here on, my climb upwards was steady. Once I started winning at badminton, my teachers were only too happy to cut me some slack. Most mornings I would arrive at school really late and on many afternoons, I'd leave by 2.30 for training. Thankfully, as I started playing more and more, neither Papa nor Mummy demanded that I study as much as I trained. That would have been impossible!

It's okay to lose once in a while

Following the district-level wins, I took part in the state-level tournaments at the Under-12 and Under-14 levels. I won most of them, but occasionally I would lose a match and that was never a nice feeling. Of course, as much as winning is sought after, losing is also part of the game. And I think it is okay to lose once in a while, just as long as it's not too often.

To be a champion you need to think like one

It was Mummy who was instrumental in making me think like a champion. I remember once asking her what the difference was between me and the World Number 1 player, and she didn't laugh at the question or think I was setting my goals too high. Instead, she looked me in the eye and told me exactly how the best player in the world was better than me. It made me feel that I could dream big, and I did begin to do so. I knew I had a lot of work ahead to get to the top, but the road was opening in front of me and I stepped on it with some confidence, thanks to Mummy.

I was lucky to have a supportive school

By the time I was in Class 7, I had made it past the state and national level tournaments and had also begun playing internationally. Between classes 8 and 10, my attendance at school dropped drastically, as I was away on tournaments so often. Each tournament would take up at least two weeks of my time, not including the time I needed to train. This was the story for those three years. That I could remain in school is all thanks to my teachers and principal. I think I have been incredibly lucky in the kind of teachers I had—they were so understanding and supportive.

When it was time for my Class 10 CBSE Board exams, I was again away playing the Junior German and Dutch Open. I made it back around twenty-five days before the exams and there was just so much to study! When the results came what a relief it was to have actually passed my 10th exams.

I want to be a professional badminton player

I was fifteen years old then and I think a lot of kids decide at that age what they would like to pursue. By this time, I too was very clear about what I wanted to become—a professional badminton player. When I told Papa this, he wasn't entirely convinced, even though I was winning tournaments and beating top players. But I think we both knew that I had steadily gone far away from the original plan of becoming a doctor.

I stopped attending school after Class 11. So yes, my academic pursuit did end abruptly, but there was no time to pause and think about it. I had gone too far ahead on my chosen path to ask myself if I wanted to change tracks. And looking back, I can truthfully say I have no regrets.

How I made it to the top

To progress in any sport, perform consistently and take your game ahead, step by step. There are no shortcuts. My roadmap was district level, state level, then national level, but my eyes were already on the international circuit. When I was twelve years old, I was part of a team event at the Commonwealth Games. I was a junior player, unranked, and therefore spent all my time on the bench. It was frustrating to be there and not play. But I was too new and thankfully, I used the time wisely, training hard and watching the others play.

I really wanted to be part of the international circuit and an opportunity came a year later, in 2003, in the Czechoslovakia

Junior Open in Prague. It was an Under-19 tournament and I played five rounds before reaching the finals, where I won gold. I was thirteen years old, still an unranked player, and yet I had just beaten players ranked between world numbers 60 and 20.

This win gave me such a burst of confidence and validated that I had what it takes to play international badminton. I started playing in the Senior Nationals when I was fifteen. My sights were set on the Uber Cup 2006. The tournament was in Jaipur and I won every single game I played. Unfortunately, as a team, we didn't reach the finals.

Despite the loss I was determined to focus on the next big tournament, the Commonwealth Games 2006. I was a standby but was prepared to play if I got a chance. Aparna (Popat) was still the best player we had, and therefore assigned to the singles event. And then she was injured! When it was certain that she would not be able to play, I went up to the team coach Vimal Kumar and said, 'Sir, I'll play the singles event.'

The qualifying rounds followed and I managed to reach the quarter-finals, but here I lost to Xing Aiying of Singapore. Still we won the bronze at the CWG, and I know I had a part to play in it.

2007—a year of tears

I followed this up with the Philippine Open, another big tournament where I won gold. If anybody thinks it was smooth sailing from here on, they're completely wrong. The following year, 2007, started well, but then March came with the All England tournament, one of the big-ticket games. I lost in the second round. I came back to India and played the All India National Games. Here I won gold again, but somehow internationally nothing was working for me. I played in Malaysia, the Philippines, Singapore, Indonesia, Japan, China, Korea, Denmark, France, Hong Kong, Chinese Taipei, Macau, Vietnam... but in every tournament I lost in the first or second round. I cried so much that year! That's what I remember 2007 as being—a year of tears. The papers wrote that my success of 2006 had been a fluke. Mummy and Papa stood by me of course, reminding me always that in sports winning and losing both hold true.

When the year ended no one could have been happier than I was. And no matter what, I look back at 2007 as the year that taught me so much about myself and my game.

Picking myself up again

In 2008, I won the Chinese Taipei Open, one of the prestigious Grand Prix tournaments, and the World Junior Championships. I also made it to the Super Series Finals in Malaysia, where I was a semi-finalist. The sluggishness of 2007, it seemed, was over and I was on a roll once more.

As it turned out, the years 2008, 2009 and 2010 were a culmination of all that I had been working towards. My ranking had shot up from 200 to 28 in two years and now I was inching towards the Top 10. In December 2008, I entered the hallowed Top 10 league.

Perhaps my best year yet was 2010, when I won the Indian Open, the Singapore Open, the Indonesian Open, the Hong

Kong Open, and to crown it all, a gold at the Commonwealth Games! What a moment that was! As the Indian national anthem played, everyone present sang it with me. I still get goosebumps when I think of it. I had won gold for India!

Finally, an Olympic medal

Each one of us dreams of playing for his or her country in the Olympics, and I am no different.

The rule allows up to fifteen top-ranked players, one from each country. The remaining players are chosen based on a quota, which is one player per country, irrespective of ranks, making it a total of sixty-four players.

My first Olympics was in 2008 at Beijing. I reached the quarter-finals where I lost to Indonesian Maria Kristin Yulianti. I was disappointed of course.

London. I was so excited to be there! When I made it to the quarter-finals, I felt more confident. I won that game in straight sets and it was a huge relief for me. Unfortunately, in the semi-final, in my hurry to win, I made several silly mistakes. The loss was devastating, as it meant that I would now lose the gold and the silver.

It was heartbreaking for me to lose, but I still had one more match to play and needed to conserve my energy and strength. I was to play Wang Xin. I picked up the lead but she came back full throttle. I made it 20-18 and could see that she was out of breath. When she tried to stand up, she fell from severe exhaustion. Still, I lost the first set to her. I was back in form and hitting well, but one point into the second set, Wang Xin gave up. She forfeited the game. The bronze was mine!

I am so happy that I returned home with a medal! The welcome I got was out of this world. This is what makes playing for the country so special!

Who am I?

I am Saina Nehwal from India, and being a player from India defines who I am. When I play, it's for my parents, my coach, and my country. The sense of patriotism I feel is very much a part of who I am. When I play, the Indian tricolour is on my T-shirt and I never forget that I am playing for my country.

12

I teach the way that I wish I was taught. The lectures are coming from me, an actual human being who is fascinated by the world around him.

SALMAN 'SAL' KHAN

∽

Khan Academy is a non-profit online educational website with the mission of providing 'free world-class education for anyone anywhere'. Founded by **Salman 'Sal' Khan** in 2006, the Khan Academy has over 10 million unique users from across the world each month.

Sal Khan holds four degrees: including an MS in computer science from Massachusetts Institute of Technology (MIT) and an MBA from Harvard Business School. A hedge fund analyst, Sal realized the practicality of posting his tutorials on YouTube, while teaching his cousin online. The popularity of his tutorials prompted him to leave his job in 2009 and dedicate himself fully to Khan Academy.

I can well imagine what Sal's family and friends thought when he decided to give up a job to create 'tutorials'. When I suddenly decided to give up my fairly cushy job as creative head of Ogilvy, and follow my passion and become a full-time quizmaster, many thought that I had lost it. Twenty years down the line I look back and realize what a wise decision it was. So, if you have a passion, and you are good at it, follow that dream, follow your heart, believe in yourself.

∽

Enjoy this Second Chance
Salman 'Sal' Khan

Giving access to free knowledge

Many of you may not remember, but in the late 1990s and early 2000s, many corporations and universities were exploring how they could profit or protect themselves from online education. Then MIT stepped in the mix and launched MIT OpenCourseWare. As powerful as the offering had the potential to be, MIT's rationale for it was even more powerful. MIT was implicitly saying that some things are more important than profit or any strategic concerns. Even if it would cost the institute potential revenues, MIT had the moral clarity to realize that if it could give access to knowledge to people around the world for free, it should and would.

I was busy working at a startup in San Francisco when the announcement came out in 2001. I had no idea then that my own life-adventure would be so closely linked, but when MIT had announced OpenCourseWare, I never felt prouder or more inspired by where I had gone to school. When others were exploring what was profitable or how to defend their existing offerings or just watched from the sidelines, MIT had the moral clarity and boldness to just do what it thought was right.

Leading by example

Many universities aspire to teach their students ethics; but nothing is more powerful than when they lead by example. This in no small way inspired what has now become the Khan Academy. And now, MIT has once again put principle over profit by spearheading edX with Harvard. For this and many, many other reasons, I am honoured to come here and thank the institution that I love so much for reminding me through its actions what is most important.

But MIT has also affected me on a more personal level. Many of my very closest friends are alumni. My wife went to MIT. The president of Khan Academy was my freshman year roommate. His wife went to MIT. One of our board members went to MIT. His wife went to MIT.

Of our many close friends from MIT, 90 per cent are married to each other. Now, I think when this many friendships and marriages coming out of one place, as romantic as the Infinite Corridor may be, it begs some introspection.

In fact, so extreme is the coupling that I have observed here that I have sometimes suspected that this whole place is just a front for a DARPA-funded human breeding project.

But I think it also goes still deeper than that.

MIT School of Wizadry

I always tell people that MIT is the closest thing to being Hogwarts—Harry Potter's wizarding school—in real life.

The science and innovation that occurs here looks no different than pure magic to most of the world. The faculty here is the real-world McGonagalls—that's you President Hockfield—and Dumbledores. There are secret tunnels and passages with strange wonders and creatures around every corner—some of whom may just finish their thesis this decade. The names of history's great wizards surround us here in Killian Court—from Aristotle to Galileo, Newton to Darwin. They remind us that we have inherited an ancient art. One that, despite being vilified or suppressed by forces of ignorance throughout history, is the prime cause of human progress and well-being.

Also like Hogwarts, MIT brings young people from around the country and world who are a little bit off-the-charts in their potential for this 'magic'. Some come from environments and communities that celebrated their gifts. Others had to actively hide their abilities and passions for fear of being ostracized and ridiculed. Students come to MIT from every religion, every ethnicity, some from educated, affluent families, others from ones that live in near poverty. But they—you, we—shared a common passion. Something that made us feel a little different. We sensed that MIT might be a place where there were others like us. Where we could challenge ourselves and develop our craft.

This is a place where students with perfect SAT scores and genius-level IQs can and will fail exams; a place where students who may have been the brightest in their school, state or country often feel mediocre and stressed; a place where sleep regularly takes a back seat to the intellectual intensity of the curriculum.

But this intensity is what forges deep bonds, honesty

and compassion. You have laughed together, comforted each other, procrastinated together and cried together. You have been with each other at your best and worst moments. Like soldiers who have fought alongside each other, you have shared experiences that the rest of the world may not understand or even comprehend.

Because of this, whenever you see another MIT graduate the rest of your life, you know that you have a past in common; that you both have secret powers that you often keep hidden from regular view. Regardless of how different your pre-MIT backgrounds may have been, you will feel deeply connected—like people meeting from a long-lost village or family or galaxy. You will actively seek other MIT people out. When others talk about an intellectually challenging experience they had or complain about how hard they had to work, you will glance at the other MIT grad in the room and share a quick smirk.

So coming here, I really feel like I have come to my roots. That I am surrounded by an incredibly good-looking family that I am deeply connected to and that I care deeply about.

Fight negativity

Many of you will soon enter the outside world and be somewhat taken aback. It will be far less efficient, far less fair, far less productive, and far more political than what you may have imagined it to be. There will be pessimism and cynicism everywhere. It is easy to succumb to this, to become cynical or negative yourself. If you do, you with the potential that you have, it would be a loss for yourself and for humanity.

To fight these forces of negativity, to increase the net positivity in the world, to optimize the happiness of yourself and the people you love, here are some tips and tools that I like to return to. I am not too much older than most of you, so take all of this with a large grain of salt.

Show that you care

Start every morning with a smile—even a forced one—it will make you happier. Replace the words 'I have to' with 'I get to' in your vocabulary. Smile with your mouth, your eyes, your ears, your face, your body at every living thing you see. Be a source of energy and optimism. Surround yourself with people that make you better. Realize or even rationalize that the grass is truly greener on your side of the fence. Just the belief that it is becomes a self-fulfilling prophecy.

View stressful, political interactions as nothing more than a deeply immersive strategy game. One that can be won if you stay focused on what matters most and your emotions and ego are not tied to your argument.

If you find yourself arguing with someone whom you respect and love, try to surrender your own ego to the shared identity you have with that person. In the heat of an argument, do the opposite of what your pride tells you to do. If you have the self-control, stop talking and give your opponent a random, intense minute-long hug.

Make people feel that you care about them. And here's a well, a little secret—the best way to do this is to actually care about them.

Make people feel that you are listening to them. Another little secret, the best way to do this is to actually listen.

Don't be materialistic

When you gain or lose material things, remember how silly they really are. How little they mean relative to your health and relationships.

When you feel stressed, look up at the night sky and ponder the distance to the next star and the age of the universe. Think of all the other stressed sentient creatures from other star systems and galaxies looking out in the vastness of space in wonder and awe and take comfort in your shared experience.

When you feel overwhelmed, walk alone through the woods and forget your name, your title, your education and view yourself for what you really are—another mammal wondering why it is here but appreciating the fact that your civilization has not as yet been evaporated by a supernova.

Be the best you can

Try to build true empathy. Regardless of your actual spiritual beliefs, it is sometimes helpful to imagine that time is not linear; that in past or future, or I guess parallel life, you literally are, have been or will be every person. That after this life, you will go back in time and be reincarnated as the person you are arguing with, or passing judgment on (and will then have to put up with the current version of you).

Remember that real success is maximizing your internally derived happiness. It will not come from external status or money or praise. It will come from a feeling of contribution. A feeling that you are using your gifts in the best way possible.

Also remember that whom you choose as a life partner is a far more important decision than what career you choose to pursue. If you are lucky enough to have a true equal, someone who fills you with joy and emotional contentment, with whom you have deep shared values, who respects you and loves you for your innate you-ness; no superficial, external failure or conflict can faze you.

But keep in mind that if you care about someone, but not enough to commit to them, the most selfish thing you can do is not let them move on.

Money and status

Money is important for the basic necessities, and even luxuries of life. All of you will be able to buy expensive fruit and go to Sea World whenever you want to. Beyond that, and many of you will go far beyond that, money is a command over resources—including people—and should be viewed as a serious responsibility.

Like money, status can be a powerful tool. But they can both distort your reality away from true internal 'groundedness'.

Don't waste inspiration

One of my former roommates who had been a bit of a track star at MIT, and I, had finished watching *Chariots of Fire* one night at 2 a.m. I told him that it made me feel like running. He simply told me, 'Don't waste inspiration.' I reminded him that it is 2 a.m. He said, 'So what; don't waste inspiration.' I looked at him for a few seconds and realized that he was dead serious. I jumped off the couch, threw on my running shoes and took to the streets.

If you ever feel inspired, take action with it. Don't let anyone tell you why you shouldn't; at least lace up and give it a try.

Be safe... be adventurous

On a similar vein, inertia, pride or fear should never be the reason why you close your mind to opportunity.

Most of my own life, I thought I had to choose between a safe route and the adventurous. When I was your age, I was a bit skeptical of speeches like this. I thought, sure, the guy at the podium can talk about changing the world, but what about my student loans, what about my family that has worked so hard to get me here. What about all the people who pursued their dreams and failed? Wouldn't it be selfish of me to give up the secure path for the long shot at the audacious?

I can't say this to any group of young people, but for those of you graduating today, I believe that you can have both: security and adventure; bread on the table while taking your shots at the moon.

Don't give up your passions

We're at a unique point in history. Where what once required many people spending many years and many millions can now be done by a small group of inspired people from a dorm room, or in my case, a bedroom closet. Ideas can be proven before they need to be committed to. The revolutions of our generation—in business, education, social structure and even politics—are not being catalyzed by generals or politicians, but by highly empowered individuals like yourselves. The wizards of our time speak so we can see with clarity how the assumptions of previous generations no longer apply. And the revolutions often grow out of nothing more than an intense hobby, an inspired attempt at seeing if things can be rethought a little better.

So go forth with your careers, but leave space for your passions. Remember that you are much, much more than a title or a bank account. You are dancers and poets, inventors and athletes, musicians and innovators. If you give your passions room to breathe, you might find that is all they need to help you move the dial forward for everyone.

And this isn't just a commencement speaker trying to make you feel good or take weight off your shoulders. This is another member of your species who knows how badly the world needs you. Who knows that MIT graduates, like a tall person who learns to slouch to not stand out, sometimes undersell who they are, even to themselves. I am, in fact, putting weight on your shoulders because I know how scarce and important a resource you are.

A thought experiment

So with all that said, let me leave you with a thought experiment I use to help keep my priorities in check.

Imagine yourself in fifty years. You're in your early 70s, near the end of your career. You're sitting on your couch, having just watched the State of the Union holographic address by President Kardashian.

You begin to ponder your life, the career successes, how you've been able to provide for your family. You'll think of all the great moments with your family and friends. But then you start to think about all of the things you wished you had done just a little differently, your regrets. I can guess what they might be.

Sitting in 2062, you wish that you had spent more time with your children; that you had told your spouse how much you loved him or her more frequently; that you could have even one more chance to hug your parents and tell them how much you appreciate them before they passed; that you could have smiled more, laughed more, danced more and created more; that you better used the gifts you were given to empower others and make the world better.

Just as you're thinking this, a genie appears from nowhere and says, 'I have been eavesdropping on your regrets. They are valid ones. I can tell you are a good person so I am willing to give you a second chance if you really want one.' You say 'Sure' and the genie snaps his fingers.

All of a sudden you find yourself right where you are sitting today. It is June 8, 2012, at Killian Court. You are in your shockingly fit and pain-free 20-something body and begin to realize that it has really happened. You really do have the chance to do it over again... to have the same career successes and deep relationships. But, now you can optimize. You can laugh more, dance more and love more. Your parents are here again so it is your chance to love them like you wished you had done the first time. You can be the source of positivity that you wished you had been the first time around.

So now I stand here, once again deeply honoured to be here. Excited by what you, the MIT class of 2012—both undergrads and graduate students, the young wizards of our time—at a time like no other in human history will do with your second chance.

∽

We know only too well that what we are doing is nothing more than a drop in the ocean. But if the drop were not there, the ocean would be missing something.

MOTHER TERESA

Learning from Mother Teresa
Derek O'Brien

Life is what happens to you while you're busy making other plans.

JOHN LENNON

This is one of my favourite lines from one of my favourite philosophers. John Lennon was more than just an immensely successful musician. I've used it here in a dual context. First, it describes so beautifully and appropriately the life and trajectory of the woman who is the subject of this chapter: Mother Teresa. As an Albanian girl, growing up in a town that is now the capital of the Republic of Macedonia, would she ever have imagined that she would find her calling and her spiritual fortune on the streets of Kolkata, a city so far away and so distant from the Skopje she was raised in?

My second reason is more personal. It refers to my first meaningful meeting with Mother Teresa—my encounter with greatness if I may put it thus. It touched me and my circumstances in a way that was never expected or planned. I like to believe it changed my life, but more of that later.

What is Mother Teresa doing in a book on tips on how to

be successful? After all, she wasn't a conventional achiever. She left behind no vast properties, award-winning books or sizeable bank balance. Yet, it is a fact that she was very good at what she did—charitable works, looking after the destitute and leading a multinational organization (the Missionaries of Charity).She ran the institution with an iron grip and an easy smile while ever focused on her goals. If you analyse the methods and tools she used to achieve this, you would begin to think of her differently.

Destiny brought Mother Teresa to Kolkata, but once she started the Missionaries of Charity, Mother left nothing to chance. Mother was meticulous and focused, she planned every move and she used every relationship. She did this not for personal gain but in the service of the poor, the ill and the forsaken. *Leadership Skills of Mother Teresa* and *Management Techniques of Mother Teresa*: these are books waiting to be written.

Mother Teresa and I had two things in common—both of us lived in Kolkata and both of us were Catholic. Yet, I wasn't drawn to her because of my Christian faith. Growing up in a household where going to church was as important as being part of the neighbourhood Durga Puja committee or visiting one of my father's closest friends, a Muslim, for Id, I took God seriously but not religious identities. Like others in the city—and the world—I had admired Mother's work and the selfless service of her order of nuns, little women in their blue and white saris, literally picking up the poor, the starving and the near dead from the footpaths of Kolkata.

II

It was 1991. Mother Teresa and service to humanity were far from my mind. I was at an inflection point in my life and had just taken a major if controversial decision—controversial for my parents at least. After eight and a half years in advertising, I had decided to quit Ogilvy & Mather. For the last three years, while I worked as the creative head, I had spent most of my weekends conducting quizzes. I had done that to fulfil a childhood obsession with trivia and strange facts and to earn some money on the side. Somehow, I felt there was scope for a company that would leverage this quizzing expertise and build a business around the pursuit of knowledge... *making knowledge interesting to help people and brands grow.*

My parents and friends were not so sure. They couldn't understand why I wanted to give up a steady job and couldn't fathom this crazy entrepreneurial bug that had bitten me. Nevertheless, I was determined to give it a shot, to make my hobby my profession. Were there moments of self-doubt? Oh yes, there were several. I took three months off between Ogilvy & Mather and Big Ideas—the new company that I was setting up—and decided to spend it not winning new contracts and deals but doing something meaningful. I didn't know what I wanted to do but somewhere deep inside I wanted time for contemplation and to pay back my dues.

One day, the photographer Sunil K. Dutt came to see me. I had known him for several years. He was older than me and renowned as a chronicler of Kolkata and its many moods. Sunil came with an idea. He had a set of black-and-white pictures of Kolkata that he wanted to sell to a publisher for a book. Could I help him? A book on Kolkata ... This set me thinking. Could I take up the project myself and publish it under my own imprint? It would be a fun project, and would help me do something to commemorate the city I so loved and which had given me so much. Sunil left the photographs with me and asked me to choose the best ones for a book. He trusted my judgement and was insistent only on the fee: ₹1,50,000.

I went through the photographs and while Sunil's work was remarkable, the pictures didn't convey anything new. Kolkata is a well-chronicled city. There have been several books and pictorial works dedicated to it. Sunil's photographs did little to contribute a new angle or give the city a new look. They were artistic frames, shot in black-and-white, but would that be enough for a book?

When Sunil and I met again, I was frank with him. He looked crestfallen. 'I need the money,' he said, 'I need that 1,50,000 rupees.' 'Why, Sunilda?' I asked him, 'that's a lot of money, why do you need it?' The answer was a punch straight in my solar plexus: 'Derek, I need the money to pay for my daughter's wedding.' Here was a man, an artiste, who had spent a lifetime worshipping his camera and his subject and not caring for currency notes. Now he needed those notes for his beloved daughter's wedding and had nothing, no assets, other than the photographs he had taken over the years. He was desperate to monetise them, to convert those photographs into a teller machine that would give him the money for the most important event in his life: his little girl's wedding.

III

I was looking for something meaningful to do, an act that would make a difference. I had found it. 'Sunilda,' I said, 'the book will be done and the wedding will go through, don't worry.' I told him the Kolkata book wasn't a good idea, however. Then I had a brainwave and asked him to show me pictures of a woman he had been chasing, stalking, following for decades: Mother Teresa. Was there a book there?

Sunil brought his collection of Mother Teresa's photographs—black-and-white works, some ordinary, some stunning and some absolute masterpieces. There was Mother praying, Mother helping a stricken child, Mother supervising cooking in a gruel kitchen, even Mother coming out of a police station, having secured the release of poor folk who had been detained unfairly. Instinctively, I knew we had a book.

The first thing I did was to take out ₹1,50,000 from the provident fund I had withdrawn from Ogilvy & Mather and give it to Sunil. Then I wondered how I could make the book stand out, for there was no dearth of books on Mother Teresa either. Discussing it with Sunil one day, I thought loudly: 'We need good captions for the photographs ... Why not get Mother to write the captions?' So on a whim and a prayer, I asked for an appointment with Mother Teresa, reaching her office in the Kolkata bylane that housed the worldwide headquarters of the Missionaries of Charity.

It was my first visit to Mother House. On the main door outside was a nameplate saying 'Mother Teresa', with an option: 'IN' or 'OUT'. If she was at home the 'OUT' was covered by a small shutter, or the other way round. Incidentally, after Mother's death in September 1997, the entrance to Mother House (where she is now buried) still always has the sign saying: 'Mother Teresa … IN'.

I broached the subject of the book to Mother Teresa. She was dismissive. Why another book? 'It will help spread the word of your work to people,' I offered. She smiled back, compassionate and clinical at the same time. 'Son, God has been good. People already know about our work.' I told her I was planning to get the book sponsored and have the sponsor donate ₹5,00,000 to the Missionaries of Charity. I would not make any money on the book. All we needed were her blessings, and her text for the captions.

Mother looked in the direction of one her colleagues, Sister Priscilla. Then she nodded, but said she had no time to write the captions. 'I have said so much over the years,' she pointed out, 'why don't you use those in the book.' It was a green signal for the project, but it meant more work for me. I would have to pore over hundreds of articles and books and speeches relating to Mother Teresa to find appropriate quotes and lines she had uttered. As I was leaving, Sister Priscilla told me what had won Mother's heart. 'So many books have been written about Mother,' she said, 'but this is first time somebody has offered something to the Missionaries of Charity.'

IV

I had to find a sponsor, somebody who would underwrite a book that had Mother Teresa's photographs described in

Mother Teresa's words. Eventually, Citibank agreed. It would give ₹5,00,000 to the Missionaries of Charity and pay for the printing and production of the book. It would also have the right to write the introduction. Jaithirth 'Jerry' Rao, now a well-regarded businessman, social entrepreneur and public intellectual but back then the India head of Citibank, agreed to sponsor the book and to write the introduction.

I worked on picking the captions and matching them with the photographs we had chosen. The designing of the book started and we went into the technicalities of choosing the paper and the printer. Then, as the book was set to go to print, Citibank phoned us. Jerry Rao would no longer be writing the introduction; the Citibank Asia head, based in Hong Kong, would be doing so. A few days later, there was another change. The Citibank international chief, based in New York, would be writing the introduction. Clearly, Mother Teresa's appeal ran across continents.

Finally, the big day came. The book was to be released by Mother Teresa in the presence of the Citibank top brass, including the India head from Bombay and the Asia head from Hong Kong. They had come with the cheque; they had also come as pilgrims to the shrine of Mother Teresa, Kolkata's living saint. Sunil K. Dutt arrived. The tennis player Naresh Kumar and his wife Sunita, among Mother's closest confidantes, were there. All of us reached the Mother House and waited for Mother to come out.

She didn't.

Word was sent. Sister Priscilla went in and then I walked

up to Mother's room, nervous and sweating, and requested her to come to the book release. Her response took me aback. 'What book?' she asked. I mumbled and stammered and told her about the photographs and the captions and our previous meeting. 'The Citibank officials are here, Mother,' I said, almost beseeching her. 'They would like you to bless them and accept that cheque…' Mother smiled. It was a naughty, childlike smile: 'I'm sure we can ask them for an ambulance, can't we? After all, it's all God's work.'

So the great lady walked out, greeted those gathered, unpacked the first copy of the book, accepted the cheque and thanked all of us, particularly the Citibank visitors. Then she added, almost as a parting shot, 'I'm sure our friends can help us with an ambulance too, for the service of the sick.' The Citibank executive from Hong Kong agreed at once. She had no choice!

V

It all ended well. The book was released to critical acclaim. The Citibank officials went home walking on air. Sunilda's daughter got married. The Missionaries of Charity got ₹5,00,000 and a spanking new ambulance to continue their work. As for me, I was happy that my three-month interlude had resulted in something useful and in a project that had proved beneficial to a variety of people in a variety of ways. I'm not much of a believer but I did feel touched by Mother's presence. I continued to call on her and attributed at least some of my professional luck thereafter to her warm wishes.

This chapter is not about me and to be fair not even about

Mother Teresa. It is about the ingredients of success. Looking back at the episode, I was struck by Mother Teresa's astuteness and negotiating skills. In her quiet, understated and unassuming way, she had taught me a lot about how to run a business, how to reach your goals and how to achieve success. Consider the evidence:

- In telling me that enough books had been written about her and that people already knew about her work, Mother portrayed a confident person who knew her 'brand equity'. She began the process of negotiation by putting me on the defensive.
- In telling me she had no time to write the captions but was happy to have me use words and quotes from her previous public appearances, Mother was displaying an acute sense of time management and core competency. Writing captions and choosing phrases was not her job, she had other things to do. These were part of my core skill and if I wanted to drive the book project, I would have to labour for it. Mother Teresa would provide food to those who needed it; she would not give me a free lunch.
- In her cultivated nonchalance and sudden request for an ambulance at the book release, again she was taking everyone in the room by surprise. This was and remains a key weapon in any transaction or interaction—surprise. Realizing she was crucial to the event and that the visitor from Hong Kong had come especially to see her, she pushed the envelope and asked for an ambulance. What's more, she knew she would succeed. She knew it even before she started.

- She did all this not for personal profit but to pay dividends to the wider stakeholders of her enterprise—her multinational corporation of compassion—the poor and the forsaken, the indigent and the destitute.
- Recalling that experience from nearly a quarter-century ago still gives me the goose bumps. To me, it defines success and Mother Teresa exemplifies achievement. It was all her achievement, all done her way.

Acknowledgements

To Andrew Scolt, Sudeshna Shome Ghosh, and all my colleagues at Derek O'Brien & Associates... Thank you for making it happen.—Derek

∽

The publisher and editor gratefully acknowledge the following for their permission to reprint:

HarperCollins *Publishers* India for permission to excerpt from *A Shot at History* by Abhinav Bindra with Rohit Brijnath. Reproduced in arrangement with HarperCollins *Publishers* India from the book *A Shot at History* published by them © Abhinav Bindra. Unauthorized copying is strictly prohibited.

The piece 'Success Comes from Will-power' by Akio Morita is from *Made in Japan* by Akio Morita and Edwin M. Reingold, and Mitsuko Shimomura, copyright © 1986 by E.P. Dutton. Used by permission of Dutton, a division of Penguin Group (USA) LLC.

A.P.J. Abdul Kalam to excerpt from *My Journey: Transforming Dreams into Actions* (Rupa Publications India, 2013).

Azim Premji to excerpt from his speech delivered at the Indian Institute of Technology, Madras in 2001.

Devi Shetty to excerpt from his speech delivered at S.D.M. College of Medical Sciences, Karnataka, in 2007.

'Never Give Up' by Donald Trump is excerpted from *Trump Never Give Up: How I Turned My Biggest Challenges into Success* by Donald Trump, reproduced with permission of John Wiley & Sons, Inc.

Leander Paes to excerpt from his speech delivered at the Mind Rocks Youth Summit organized by the India Today Group in 2013.

HarperCollins *Publishers* India for permission to excerpt from *Think Like a Champion* by Rudy Webster. Reproduced in arrangement with HarperCollins *Publishers* India.

Rajdeep Sardesai to excerpt from his interview with M.S. Dhoni, published in ESPN CricInfo.

N.R. Narayana Murthy to excerpt from his pre-commencement lecture at the New York University (Stern School of Business) to the Class of 2007.

Penguin Books India Pvt. Ltd. to excerpt from *Playing to Win* by Saina Nehwal (Penguin India, 2012).

Salman 'Sal' Khan to excerpt from his commencement address at Massachusetts Institute of Technology, 2012.

www.ingramcontent.com/pod-product-compliance
Lightning Source LLC
Chambersburg PA
CBHW050909160426
43194CB00011B/2338